Translating Affective Neuroscience into Clinical and Educational Practice

This book is an accessible guide to understanding emotion through the lens of neuroscience. It provides a practical, developmentally informed framework with tools to translate affective neuroscience into everyday practice.

The author introduces a neuroscience-informed model of emotion grounded in the body–brain connection, explaining the theory of affective neuroscience and including practical strategies for use in both therapeutic and educational settings. Drawing on foundational work by Panksepp, Damasio, Craig, and others, the book emphasizes how seven core emotional systems drive human behavior, development, and individual agency. Describing the development and application of the Affective Inventory, it provides clinician-facing steps and reflective exercises. Through clear explanations, engaging examples, and powerful clinical insights, this book reveals how our body and brain work together to shape feeling, behavior, and connection, helping readers navigate emotion with compassion, clarity, and confidence. Downloadable client handouts are provided for practitioners and educators.

Translating Affective Neuroscience into Clinical and Educational Practice: Body, Brain, and Emotions will appeal to clinical psychologists, neuropsychologists, school psychologists, therapists, and counselors, as well as graduate students of neuroscience and neuropsychology, and education professionals.

Elaine Fletcher-Janzen, EdD, NCSP, ABPdN, is a board-certified pediatric neuropsychologist and a nationally certified school psychologist. She is a professor, clinician, and author with over 40 years of experience in training professionals in neuropsychology, school psychology, and clinical practice. She is internationally recognized for translating affective neuroscience into practical tools for educational and clinical practice.

First published 2027
by Routledge
605 Third Avenue, New York, NY 10158

and by Routledge
4 Park Square, Milton Park, Abingdon, Oxon, OX14 4RN

Routledge is an imprint of the Taylor & Francis Group, an informa business

ISBN: 978-1-041-25224-5 (hbk)
ISBN: 978-1-041-25013-5 (pbk)
ISBN: 978-1-003-74568-6 (ebk)

DOI: 10.4324/9781003745686

Typeset in Sabon
by Newgen Publishing UK

Visit the Support Material: www.routledge.com/9781041250135

Translating Affective Neuroscience into Clinical and Educational Practice

Body, Brain, and Emotions

Elaine Fletcher-Janzen EdD, NCSP, ABPdN

Routledge
Taylor & Francis Group
NEW YORK AND LONDON

First published 2027
by Routledge
605 Third Avenue, New York, NY 10158

and by Routledge
4 Park Square, Milton Park, Abingdon, Oxon, OX14 4RN

Routledge is an imprint of the Taylor & Francis Group, an informa business

ISBN: 978-1-041-25224-5 (hbk)
ISBN: 978-1-041-25013-5 (pbk)
ISBN: 978-1-003-74568-6 (ebk)

DOI: 10.4324/9781003745686

Typeset in Sabon
by Newgen Publishing UK

Visit the Support Material: www.routledge.com/9781041250135

To David, Emma, Zach, Leif, and Tara with my whole heart.

Contents

Preface

Necessity is often the mother of invention, and this book was born from necessity. It grew out of my work with children and adolescents recovering from brain injuries and chronic illnesses, where healing required more than cognitive rehabilitation. In every case, the task was to help the child reconnect the body with the sense of self and agency. Traditional models of neuropsychology and intervention, focused primarily on cognition and behavior, proved insufficient for addressing the real struggles that children and families faced. The missing link was emotion: Not simply as a psychological construct, but as a biological process rooted in the body's effort to stay safe, connected, and in balance.

As a school psychologist, university educator, diplomate in pediatric neuropsychology, I began to recognize that many of the challenges labeled as "behavioral" or "executive" were actually expressions of dysregulated emotional circuitry. The children in my practice taught me, again and again, that emotion precedes thought. Long before a student can concentrate, a child can learn, or a family can problem-solve, the brain must feel safe. Over time, it became clear that the brain's architecture for learning and adaptation is built upon the body's emotional foundations.

This realization led me into the emerging field of affective neuroscience, where outstanding researchers such as Jaak Panksepp, Antonio Damasio, A. Bud Craig, and others have catalyzed a paradigm shift in our understanding of human emotion. Their pioneering work reframed affect as the organizing force of consciousness as a primary biological process that guides cognition, behavior, and relationships. Panksepp's identification of the seven core emotional systems, together with Craig's and Damasio's (and others) elucidation of interoceptive pathways and somatic feeling, gave scientific form to what clinicians have long observed: Emotion is not the opposite of reason, it is its foundation.

From this intersection of science and practice, *Translating Affective Neuroscience* took shape. It arose from the necessity of helping clinicians, educators, and families make sense of complex neuroscience and transform it into practical tools for supporting regulation, learning, and resilience. The model presented in this book invites readers to view emotion not as a latent problem to be managed, but as essential biological data: Signals from the body that reveal what the nervous system needs to restore balance, safety, and connection.

This work also represents a broader movement in the human sciences. It also represents a paradigm shift away from viewing emotion as secondary or disruptive, and toward recognizing it as central to development, adaptation, and well-being. It reflects an ongoing dialogue between research and real life, between the laboratory and the therapy room, between the child's lived body experiences and the clinician's attuned mind.

In this sense, *Translating Affective Neuroscience* is both a translation and an integration. It offers clinicians and educators a framework grounded in empirical science yet deeply human in spirit. It also stands as part of the larger paradigm shift led by affective neuroscientists: one that restores feeling to its rightful place at the heart of what it means to think, learn, and be alive.

In terms of acknowledgments, I should inform the reader that I used ChatGPT (Version-5.1) in the editing process. It saved countless hours of my fiddling with table margins, APA style issues, spelling, grammar, and abstracts for publication. Notwithstanding, I am still responsible for all formatting, meaning, and content. I should also note that the references cited at the end of each chapter are greatly reduced from the literature that culminated the final ideas for the book. Citing all reference works that I have read in the past six years that led up to this point would have diminished the readability. Therefore, those references that are listed are representative not conclusive. Readers who wish to read deeper or original work should pursue the major authors (and the shoulders of whom they stood) cited in Chapter 5: Reading their work in their voices is simply stunning.

Translating Affective Neuroscience is the culmination of over 40 years of clinical practice. As to who to thank for bringing this book to life, there are too many to name from too many years! However, my first thought is to state that I have a deep feeling of gratitude to the clients who trusted me to hold the space for their pain and who shared the joy of their accomplishments with me. I am in awe of their courage and fortitude.

I am also grateful for my colleagues over the years, especially Dr. Pip McGirl, Dr. Margaret Semrud-Clikeman, and Ellen Murphy who put up with my endless prattling about paradigm shifts for years and were kind enough to give me honest feedback.

I have to apologize to my family for the exhaustive "ah ha" moments that kept on popping up at inappropriate times. Fortunately, those moments are over now so it is safe to eat dinner with me again! Seriously, thank you for your tireless support it means the world to me.

Lastly, I would like to thank the editorial team at Routledge, in particular the delightful Hannah Rich, for taking a chance on this work: I appreciate their courage, expertise, and tenacity!

Elaine Fletcher-Janzen, Ed.D., NCSP, ABPdN
Niles, Michigan
December 12, 2025

Part I

Translating Affective Neuroscience Theory

Chapter 1

Introduction and Theory

For much of modern history, emotions have been essentially treated as unpredictable storms and things to be weathered, controlled, or overcome in the name of reason. In psychology, education, and even in parenting and therapy, emotions have often been seen as irrational forces in the personality of an individual that interfere with learning, behavior, or maturity. But a growing amount of research in affective neuroscience invites us to rethink that assumption entirely.

This book starts from a different place and emphasizes the body. Emotions are not just feelings that happen in our minds: they are full-body experiences grounded in biology. Our brains are in constant communication with our internal organs, tissues, and systems, sensing subtle shifts in pressure, temperature, energy, and need. This process, called interoception, is the foundation of emotional life. What we call "feelings" are actually interpretations of internal states designed to help us survive, connect, predict, and adapt.

Affective neuroscience shows us that emotions are not messy leftovers from an earlier stage of evolution. They are built-in biological tools that help regulate the body, guide behavior, and build social bonds. The latest neuroscientific research suggests that core emotions such as seeking, rage, fear, panic/grief, care, play, and lust have an essential and practical function. Emotions are not random or ornamental responses. They are organized, patterned biological systems that evolved to serve critical roles in survival, attachment, and learning.

Rather than resisting the idea that emotions are foundations to thinking, this book invites us to listen to them at all times. Emotions offer crucial information about what matters to us, what we need, and how we are doing. They are signals to and from our bodies that something in our internal or external environment requires attention. In this way, emotions are more than reactions: they are messages.

The structure of the book mirrors the shift from disconnection to understanding. It begins with a broad overview of how the brain and body process emotion and introduces a more integrated model of affective experience. From there, it explores each of the core emotion systems in depth, offering insight into their neuroanatomy, neurochemistry, and functional roles. The book then turns toward application and how clinicians, educators, and caregivers can work with emotional systems in a grounded, respectful, and compassionate way.

This approach is both biologically informed and deeply humanistic. It honors the science of emotion while holding space for each person's unique story. It recognizes that while emotional

DOI: 10.4324/9781003745686-2

systems are universal, their expression is shaped by culture, history, attachment, genes, trauma, and neurodiversity.

Ultimately, this book is not about controlling emotions but about understanding them. It offers a framework for seeing emotions not as obstacles to well-being, but as essential guides. It asks us to move beyond outdated mind–body separation and to appreciate the wisdom of the whole person with the brain, body, and heart working together.

In these pages, the reader will not find a manual for suppressing emotion or achieving a narrow idea of "emotional regulation". Instead, the reader will find a roadmap for emotional agency and the ability to recognize, interpret, and respond to emotions in ways that support connection, safety, and growth. This is an invitation to see emotion not as something to be managed, but as something to be trusted.

Zeitgeist of the Times

Affective neuroscience is an area of neuroscience that is rapidly infiltrating all other areas of inquiry and is definitely leading a new way of thinking. It is the study of how the brain–body creates, identifies, and translates emotions into actions. It looks at the brain circuits, body systems, and neurochemicals involved in feelings like hunger, pain, fear, care, play, anger, and sadness. This relatively new field helps us understand how brain–body shapes behavior, relationships, mental health, and development and how these emotional systems are wired into our biology from before birth.

International efforts in pedagogical neuroscience research are in full flush and hundreds of articles are coming out every year that explore the mind–body connection in behavior and learning. Unfortunately, much of the research is so detailed and so down in the weeds that it is difficult to see how most of it can help ourselves or other people. There are also popular science books, outside the area of affective neuroscience, that are very broad or superficial and some that misrepresent current knowledge about emotions. Whether it be a school curriculum, social-emotional training, advertising gimmick, music, or clicks on social media many resources on emotions are now including information about the brain. At best, non-neuroscientific books make people aware about the brain and optimistic about learning. At worst, they give misinformation and lead people down disappointing or potentially harmful roads. Clinicians and educators have watched these trends unfold in both academic and therapeutic settings and now is the time for course correction based on evidence that translates into real-life applications.

The study of the brain and its relation to the body is complicated at best! One scientist is researching this section of the brain, and another scientist is researching another and no one gets to study the whole thing. Making sense of fragmented pieces of research and bringing them to a place where we can all benefit needs translators. Indeed, there is a whole area of funding provided by the Federal government for "translational research". Instead of research results staying in a stuffy article or the laboratory we want the results to help us live our daily lives. This is the purpose of translational neuroscience, to take what we know about the research on the brain and bring the mind–body into everyday life. The information in this book is a summary of hundreds of well-designed and relevant studies that provide us with a wonderful window into how mammals use emotions to support survival. It is also a close translation of these studies into a cohesive set of practical counseling applications for individuals, families, groups, and systems. However, we must keep in mind that research and its translation is confined to the limits of the writers being naturally swayed by their history, training, funding, the zeitgeist of the times, and the status of what we know.

Theory to Practice

There is no such thing as an objective researcher or practitioner. We come to research with a set of values and training that shape our view of humanity, and we learn our trade from people who are entrenched in their own biases. This is ok. This is human. However, we must keep that in mind when designing research and practice translation parameters, we must question our biases and question the biases of others. As long as we have awareness about our basic values, we can build in structures that help us stay objective as possible within the confines of the scientific method. After all, we are mandated to "do no harm" and so we try to base our practice on a compendium of theories and rigorously designed research that hopefully flows into positive results.

We also need to be aware that popular theories about human emotions are reflective of the times in which they appear. Psychology, neuropsychology, and neuroscience have gone through many periods where philosophers, scientists, and religious entities have expounded on the nature of man and how emotions play a role in our human existence. Of course, there is no one true explanation. The emphasis in the last sentence is on the word "true". True is a nebulous term and is best left up to those who seek it. As for this author, and most scientists, all we try to strive to do is add a bit of light to the sum of what is known. Theories are wonderful tools for codifying all of what we know about a subject and then trying to get it into a cohesive form. Theories, then, should lead scientists on where to go next. But what if the theory is based on poor research? Or on erroneous assumptions? Or outdated tools for living? then what we will receive is a well-intentioned but flawed understanding of emotions and that will lead to poor or ineffective outcomes for those we are trying to help. Hence, it is up to us all to challenge assumptions that influence theories, challenge theories that drive research, and push ourselves to see beyond the past and test the limits of innovation. This is the mission of the field of affective neuroscience.

What Is Affective Neuroscience?

Basically, the field of affective neuroscience has a special place within the general field of neuroscience. It has been considered to be a niche area of study. However, the definition of what is an emotion has broadened considerably and now includes constructs such as motivation, default mode network, and neuromodulation of sensory information. Science moves slowly, and cognitive neuroscience, which ranges from genetics to learning, has dominated the research world for the past 30 years. It is more focused on brain mechanisms and does not generally seek to see the individual in the real world. Therefore, it is quite difficult for us to translate cognitive neuroscientific studies into practical interventions. Of course, the minute emotions come into the picture (literally in neuroimaging), the picture starts to get pretty fuzzy. In some respects, emotions are problematic for a researcher. They seem so subterranean and ethereal. They also seem wily and unpredictable and that goes against what most scientists want: predictability. Can we predict when people are going to experience anger, compassion, play, or fear? Well, yes, but only to a certain degree and there is the quandary for researchers: they need more certainty to be able to take their results to push the field forward.

Affective neuroscience can be considered a relatively new field, and the academic world is vying for a dominant theory. There are some who believe that the brain makes up emotions as it adjusts to the demands of the environment and there are few or no innate or discrete biological emotions that have evolved during the centuries of modern man (e.g. Barrett, 2017). There are others who study us mammals from a biopsychosocial perspective and trace emotions from deeper (and more innate) parts of the brain all the way up to consciousness (e.g. Craig, 2014; Damasio, 1994; Panksepp & Biven, 2012). The latter do not dismiss the former but the former dismisses the later. This academic battle is therefore one-sided and probably reflective of the zeitgeist of our times and includes the academic politics of where to get funding for conducting research.

One wonderful piece of news that will affect us all from now forward, is that an international effort to codify and unify research on emotions was launched in 2015 and in 2024 the Human Affectome was finally presented to the world (Schiller et al, 2024). This effort by over 170 international neuroscientists in 23 countries incorporates all research to date and defines what we mean by affective neuroscience. It also directs where future research will be going. So, the field of affective neuroscience is now defined and global! The importance of this product is immense. We can now look forward to more of an unbiased and open field that will represent culturally sensitive and practical research. One thing is for sure, affective neuroscience offers an integrative and body-aware science of emotion and that is long overdue for translation into applied settings.

The Neuroscientific Basis for This Book: Translated Tools for Living

The wellspring for this book was the culmination of my scientific and clinical practice taking a new tack. The new direction was not so much directional as my making connections between the latest events in affective neuroscience and their immediate usefulness in counseling and differential diagnosis. It forced translation because it made so much sense and significantly contributed to my being more effective as a consultant, trainer, and clinician. When I use affective neuroscience in a psychoeducational manner with clients, school teams, and families, the responses are immediate and positive. It speaks strongly because it affirms lived experiences and is easy to understand. I developed the Affective Inventory to streamline an assessment of the client's emotions from a brain–body perspective and to create a tool that would enhance rapport and educate at the same time.

The theory behind the Inventory method (explained in Chapter 5) is predominantly based on Jaak Panksepp's view that emotions are ancestral tools for living (Panksepp & Biven, 2012). They live deep in the brain and act as catalysts for change or adaption. According to Panksepp, there are seven basic innate emotions that have their own specific pathways from the body to the brain and back: RAGE, CARE, LUST, SAD, PLAY, SEEKING, AND FEAR (they are capitalized here to make them distinct constructs). They are deeply subcortical, and we learn from infancy onwards to articulate these emotions clearer and clearer as we get more mature. When I say that these basic emotions live deep in the brain, I mean that they are not initially felt in areas that have language or reasoning. We become aware of them by consciously acknowledging that our body is feeling something that needs attention.

There are homeostatic emotions like hunger, thirst, temperature and we will at some point recognize a body feeling and say something to ourselves or others "wow, its hot in here!" or "I'm hungry let's get something to eat!". There are also social emotions like the seven just mentioned that are more about how we navigate our way through real-life. We see someone being mean to someone else and we feel anger, or we feel delight when we see a loved one. First, we feel the emotion as a bodily sensation then we feel it consciously and can describe it with language (verbal and nonverbal). Sometimes it's just a second between feeling the emotion and its emergence in our consciousness (e.g. seeing a snake on a hiking trail) and other times, we need some time to sort through exactly what our body is telling us and we need to check things out a few times before figuring out what to do with the emotion (e.g. not sure if someone is being sincere and how to handle it).

It is important to remember that we usually are having multiple emotions at one time, and that they can be conflicting. All day long we are making choices that involve emotions and the more we consciously know about what we like (approach), or we don't like (avoidance) the better we can manage our days and life. Most of the time our emotions are not activating us to do something dramatic. Most of the time they help us figure out tiny decisions. At other times they can be monumental and very strong in the body. Usually, we keep the powerful level of emotions for very important events such as empathizing with a friend, loving our children as we watch them sleep, defending our bodies if we get physically attacked, experiencing profound grief when we lose a loved one. Each of the seven emotions are therefore experienced on a continuum from mild to intense depending on what job we need to get done.

Again, emotions are tools, and we use them to help us navigate what we want out of the day and what we want out of life. In fact, there is research that indicates that without emotions we cannot make decisions. We can have all the facts in the world, but without an emotion body memory about what the choices mean, we cannot predict the outcome of any course of action (Damasio, 1994; 1999). Emotions are shortcuts to help us make decisions. They come racing up from the body memories deep in the brain powered by neurotransmitters and neurohormones and give us incredibly quick understanding of what we feel comfortable doing in any given moment. This is self-empowerment! This is human agency!

Why Write This Book Now?

At the time of this writing, I am unaware of any book on the market that translates current affective neuroscience into a parsimonious therapeutic tool that is theory, research, and clinically based to be used in individual, group, families, and school systems. This approach is deeply embedded in the human mind–brain and yet can be easily understood by children and adults alike.

Basically, this book's time is now because there is now enough affective research to significantly change the way we think about emotions. We have the scientific base that urges us to feel uncomfortable with the traditional ways of thinking about emotions they because they do not fit anymore. We have reached a tipping point when we need a new overarching paradigm to guide our practice. We also live in a time when self-help and social-emotional skills training is at its height in our culture. We also know that what we have being doing to date in the public schools is not working as well as we would like because social-emotional programming is usually underfunded, sequestered from main instruction, and is not considered to be an integral part of academic success. This programming also starts with a false base in that it relies on an old paradigm that does not rest on a biopsychosocial model.

There are many traditional books on the market on emotions, social-emotional learning, self-help etc. and they all seek to help us understand how we function and learn to live a more enjoyable life. Some are based on research, some are not. Some easy to read, and some are detailed tomes that emphasize technical aspects of brain functioning that are difficult to understand or translate.

This book is hopefully an easy to read and practical book that will help clinicians and families traverse traditional ways of thinking about emotions to more current ideas. In general, the journey would be from thinking about emotions as irrational, unreliable, sidebars to behavior and shifting to the belief that emotions are embodied smart-tools that are essential for survival.

To support this shift scientifically, research on interoception and homeostatic regulation has shown that emotions are an integral part of every choice we make in our waking hours. Without emotions we actually make poorer decisions and are less rational. We cannot escape using emotions all the time because we are wired to receive sensory information about what is good and what is no good for us at any given moment from the body up to the brain and back again in a loop. All day, every day.

Research studies on constructs within affective neuroscience, such as interoception (the ability to sense internal bodily signals such as heart rate, respiration, and gut sensations) consistently shows that individuals with higher interoceptive awareness tend to experience stronger emotional clarity, greater empathy, and improved emotion regulation (Craig, 2014; Critchley & Garfinkel, 2017; Damasio, 1994; 1999). Training programs that enhance interoceptive sensitivity, such as mindfulness and somatic awareness exercises, are associated with increased resilience to stress, reduced anxiety, and improved self-regulation (e.g. Mahler, 2015; Somatic Experiencing International, 2025). Interoceptive accuracy is linked to physiological markers like heart rate variability, that reflect the body's capacity to adaptively respond to emotional challenges (Critchley & Garfinkel, 2017). Clinical evidence suggests that disruptions in interoception contribute to emotional dysregulation in conditions like anxiety, depression, and trauma.

Interventions that restore interoceptive functioning can support recovery by reconnecting individuals to the felt sense of their emotions and body states, fostering emotional insight and regulation. This is a dynamic adjustment in traditional thought about emotion. The latest affective neuroscientific research suggests, without a doubt, that we should be very much in touch with our emotions because they provide very important data about what this human biological organism needs to survive and not only survive but thrive.

Affective neuroscience has been firmly established as a distinct area of neuroscience, it has achieved an international organizational framework, and studies are showing that translating the brain–body is a valid process for effective outcomes. Why write this book now? It's time to change and shift direction on how we all feel about the feels. Instead of suppressing what is inside of us to adhere to our cultural training, we must start delving deep inside and living true to our personal and professional goals and dreams. It is time for affective neuroscience to help us find the way.

References

Barrett, L. F. (2017). *How emotions are made: The secret life of the brain*. Houghton Mifflin Harcourt.

Craig, A. D. (2014). *How do you feel? An interoceptive moment with your neurobiological self*. Princeton University Press.

Critchley, H. D., & Garfinkel, S. N. (2017). Interoception and emotion. *Current Opinion in Psychology*, 17, 7–14. https://doi.org/10.1016/j.copsyc.2017.04.020

Damasio, A. (1994). *Descartes' error: Emotion, reason, and the human brain*. G. P. Putnam's Sons.

Damasio, A. (1999). *The feeling of what happens: Body and emotion in the making of consciousness*. Harcourt.

Mahler, K. J. (2015). *Interoception: The eighth sensory system*. AAPC Publishing.

Panksepp, J., & Biven, L. (2012). *The archaeology of mind: Neuroevolutionary origins of human emotions*. W. W. Norton.

Schiller, D., Lowe, L., Becker, S., & Cromwell, H. (2024). *The human affectome project: Mapping emotion to brain and behavior*. Springer.

Somatic Experiencing International. (2025). *Somatic experiencing research and training resources*. https://traumahealing.org

Chapter 2

History and Development of Affective Neuroscience

History of Emotions

From Passions to Pathology

The study of emotions has evolved significantly over time, integrating (or reflecting) insights from philosophy, psychology, neuroscience, and other disciplines. The history of the study of emotions is important to know because we are entering into a paradigm shift that will require us letting go of fundamental ways of how we have thought of emotions in the past. The predominant views about emotions have always swung back and forth depending on who was telling the story, politics, religious freedom, the establishment of the scientific method, the creation of neuroscience and technology, and the current growth of affective neuroscience.

In some ways we have come full circle. In Plato and Aristotle's time, emotions were call "passiona" or passions. Socrates taught that emotions were the primary motivators of man, and that pathos and virtue was in the dealing with emotions in a way that was to be praised. Emotions were thought of as ethics and that they went as deep as the soul. Religious writers in the 13th century considered the passions to be sensory in nature and accompanied by bodily transformation. Passions also belonged to the part of the soul, they occurred naturally and were neither good nor bad (Nussbaum, 2001).

The first rumblings of emotions not being worthy of higher thought or divinity came in the 17th century. One philosopher, Rene Descartes, began a dualistic journey where emotions were considered separate from the soul and incited by the environment. Thoughts belonged to the mind; the body did not produce them. His famous quote "I think therefore I am" and similar philosophical explorations dominated European thought for hundreds of years. The mind and body were mechanisms and therefore separate from the soul, which at that time, was in the province of the Church (Damasio, 1994).

Prior to 19th century, writers distinguished between different states such as sensation, lust, affect, passion, but scientists gradually streamlined the vocabulary so it could be measured. If you want to measure something, you have to define it first, and so we entered a long period of debate about the origin of emotions and this began the eventual demise of dualism because the more we studied natural phenomena, the harder it got to dismiss human biology.

DOI: 10.4324/9781003745686-3

From Darwin to Behaviorism

Charles Darwin (Darwin, 1898) led a new foundation of emotions research in the late 1800s by saying that the bodily emotions were seen as innate and fixed biological entities that were independent of culture and panhuman. He concluded that emotions were evolutionarily honed yet trainable systems of adaptive behaviors that evolved as fast and flexible response patterns for particular environmental and social situations

Around the same time, William James (1884), joined by Lange, Locke, Hume, and others, tried to define emotions from a biological perspective and believed them to be disengaged from cognition and involuntary. Therefore, departing from the prior religiously (soul-based) influenced history, emotions were perceptions *and* cognitions. James and others concluded that without physiological sensations there would be no emotions. So, we got back in the body but the connection between the reciprocity of emotions and cognition still had a long way to go and it was not helped by the rise of behaviorism.

As psychology progressed as a field, the need to legitimize it as a science in its own right became imperative and leading scholars (e.g. Loeb, Watson, and Skinner) became convinced that methodologically rigorous investigations should be based on the weight of evidence and rooted in the study of the physical world (Moore, 2010). That unobservable constructs such as emotions could not be measured and therefore external and observable dimensions of the brain's functions lay in behaviors. The behavioral domination of the field led by Skinner and others resulted in a 40-year vacuum in attempts to understand the interoceptive experience of emotions (Panksepp, 1998).

Modern Breakthroughs

On the other hand, from the 1930s onwards there were a few neuroscientific researchers who were studying the brain in the laboratory. James Papez proposed a circuit theory of emotion and outlined what was termed the "limbic system" and the "emotional brain" again, supporting discrete differences between cognition and emotion but at least attempting to see the latent construct (Papez, 1938). Paul MacLean (1990) and others furthered exploration and began to account for multiple other regions (brain stem, frontal cortex) not essentially associated with emotion (e.g. memory) and further research showed many areas were directly linked to higher and lower brain structures. This line of study further eroded the duality between the brain and the body but was still hampered by the academic power politics at that time.

Another tack in research came in the 1960s and 1970s. Ekman and Friesen (1971) pioneered research on facial emotion recognition, and they identified facial expressions associated with happiness, sadness, anger, fear, disgust, and surprise. This area of study dominated psychology for many years and continues to be popular for those who are not associated with neuroscience.

Fast forward to the early 1980s we arrive at the "circumplex model of affect" (Russell, 1980) that placed emotions into a graph where pleasant and unpleasant emotions were balanced with how activated or deactivated the emotion was perceived. For instance, an unpleasant and deactivated state would be characterized as sad, depressed, or bored. Or a pleasant and activated state might be elated or happy. This line of research became very popular and has dominated psychology's interpretation of how emotions fit into the human experience. It also has provided an agreement between researchers that the brain and body spend a great deal of initial time and energy appraising the valance (good/bad, approach/avoid, pleasant/unpleasant) and importance of events.

It is important to note that much of neuroscience has been based on animal studies because we did not have the technology or ethical impetus to do invasive studies inside the human brain. Surgical procedures, on the other hand (e.g. removal of brain tumors) gave science an opportunity to see that when certain parts of the brain were stimulated or injured that the injuries create predictable changes in behavior or perception. Localization was everything! Mapping out the brain became the bedrock of neuroscience. Still, animal studies were the dominant method of manipulating the brain and observing the behavioral results.

The Beginning of Affective Neuroscience

The work of Jaak Panksepp on small mammals created an opening for looking at the concept of primary emotional systems in the brain and the role of brain circuits for different affective states. Indeed, he is considered to be the grandfather of affective neuroscience. We will hear a lot more about Panksepp's work throughout this book because his seminal work provides the foundation for the naming of discrete subcortical emotions that drive survival/balance and the translation into practical interventions. His description of emotional systems is also the basis for the Affective Inventory method described later in Chapter 13. Along with Panksepp, a group of researchers helped lay the groundwork for a brain-based, embodied understanding of emotion that we now call affective neuroscience.

A.D. (Bud) Craig (2009) was one of the earliest and most rigorous voices arguing that the *body* was central to emotional experience. His work on interoception, the sensing of internal bodily states, mapped how signals from the body travel to the insular cortex, forming the basis of feelings. Craig proposed a model of the sentient-self built not from abstract thought, but from a constant integration of body-based information. He helped reframe emotion as a process rooted in homeostasis and survival not just reaction, but bodily awareness.

Joseph LeDoux (2000) brought precision to our understanding of fear circuitry, distinguishing between fast, automatic threat responses (such as freezing or fleeing) and the conscious experience of fear. His mapping of amygdala and prefrontal cortex pathways clarified how fear operates at multiple levels and why trauma can bypass language or logic. LeDoux's research gave fear a scientific framework, pushing back against the idea that emotions are vague or unmeasurable.

Lisa Feldman Barrett (2017) offered a more contentious and constructionist view. She challenged the idea of fixed "basic emotions" and instead proposed that emotions are constructed, not pre-wired. According to her top-down theory, the brain uses prior experiences and predictive coding to make meaning out of sensory input, including interoception. She believes that emotions are not hardwired reflexes, but dynamic, context-sensitive events shaped by culture and individual history.

Karl Friston (2010) provided the computational scaffolding for this new view of emotions. His free energy principle and theories of predictive processing gave neuroscientists a way to understand how the brain anticipates the world to minimize surprise. In affective neuroscience, this means that emotions arise from the brain's attempts to predict internal bodily needs and regulate accordingly which is a major shift from stimulus-response models.

Richard Davidson (1998), meanwhile, asked how individual differences in emotional style could be tracked and changed. He explored the neural correlates of emotional traits and demonstrated that practices like mindfulness meditation could reshape the brain's affective landscape. Davidson's research showed that emotional habits are not just temperament but plastic. This opened the door to emotion-based interventions rooted in neurobiology.

Ralph Adolphs (2002) examined how the amygdala supports emotional and social processing. Through clinical studies of patients with brain lesions, he revealed the amygdala's role in interpreting social cues, empathy, and trust. Adolphs helped clarify that affective neuroscience is not only about internal feeling states, but about the way we understand and are understood by others.

Hugo Critchley and Sarah Garfinkel (2017) expanded the interoceptive lens by showing how autonomic signals like heart rate and breath influence emotional awareness. Their work emphasized the role of the anterior insula in integrating body states and emotional salience. This helped reinforce a central tenet of affective neuroscience: that emotion cannot be separated from the body's internal landscape.

Manos Tsakiris (2017; Tsakiris & De Preester, 2018) furthered these insights into embodiment, looking at how body ownership, interoception, and self-perception affect our emotional and social lives. Their research explores how the experience of being "in" a body affects everything from identity formation to social belonging. In this way, they link emotion not only to internal physiology but to how we relate to others in a shared world.

Together, these researchers (and many others too numerous to mention) helped launch a field that treats emotion not as a side effect of cognition, but as a biological force, developmental guide, and organizing principle for behavior, memory, and relationship. Their work helped move us from a fragmented view of emotion to one that sees it as embodied, embedded, and essential.

In many ways, affective neuroscience is still a young discipline. But the foundational contributions of these thinkers remind us that when we trace emotion back to the brain and body, we do not reduce it, we reclaim its full significance. Table 2.1 provides a condensed list of prominent researchers in affective neuroscience, along with their key areas of research and notable contributions:

Humanism is finally coming back to the zeitgeist via affective neuroscience, albeit with a behavioral hangover. There are some that still want to insist that we make emotions up only in the thinking part of the brain as a response to what is going on in the environment. Humans certainly do construct their experiences. The brain is very good at constructing narratives about what we are feeling and what we should do with the feeling, however, affective neuroscience has finally reached a level of sophistication (and funding) that it is now dominating contemporary scientific investigation. The current emphasis is on where emotions are in the brain, how the body and mind contribute to each other, and how they both operate to guide adaptive action. We can look forward to the Human Affectome Project (Schiller et al, 2022) leading future studies by mapping emotional states, identifying a wide array of human emotions, discovering how emotional states and networks interact with higher thought processes, how to "regulate" emotions, and finding out what is universal experience versus that which is more culturally shaped.

Future Developments in Affective Neuroscience

One point that should probably be made to put history in its rightful place, is that nearly all of researchers, philosophers, religious thinkers, and scientists that have been mentioned are all men with privilege, and from first world nations. It is not really hard to understand, then, why the field of emotions is based (at some level) on extrapolations of what it is to be male. As you will see in the Chapters on CARE and RAGE, in particular, basic scientific assumptions have been traditionally made by individuals who have large amounts of testosterone and vasopressin influencing their physiology and thoughts as opposed to individuals who have a majority of oxytocin and estrogen. From a neural hormone point of view (which strongly influences thoughts and emotions) history has been written by beings who tend to view the world in competitive terms and where predatory aggression is a large part of their emotional physiological frame of reference (Panksepp & Biven, 2012). We could wonder what the last century of research on emotions would be if it had been exclusively written by humans who have only small amounts of testosterone and vasopressin and large amounts of oxytocin (the love/cuddle hormone) and estrogen/progesterone? We should not underestimate this point, and it gives much food for speculation. For some reason, in its quest to be scientific by manipulating variables in an experimental way, we expect that the researcher's biases do not come in to play or are controlled

Table 2.1 Notable Affective Neuroscience Researchers

Name	Key Areas of Research	Notable Contributions
Jaak Panksepp	Primary emotional systems, subcortical affective circuits, animal models of emotion	Identified seven core emotional systems (e.g. SEEKING, FEAR, RAGE, CARE); established affective neuroscience as a field.
Antonio Damasio	Emotion and decision-making, somatic marker hypothesis, consciousness	Proposed the somatic marker hypothesis; demonstrated the role of emotion in rational behavior and consciousness.
A.D. (Bud) Craig	Interoception, pain, homeostasis, insular cortex function	Mapped interoceptive pathways to the insular cortex; proposed model of the sentient self-based on bodily awareness.
Joseph LeDoux	Fear, threat processing, amygdala function, emotional memory	Distinguished between fear behavior and conscious fear; mapped fear circuits involving the amygdala and prefrontal cortex.
Lisa Feldman Barrett	Constructed emotion theory, predictive coding, emotion variability	Challenged basic emotion theory; proposed that emotions are constructed through prediction and social context.
Karl Friston	Predictive coding, free energy principle, brain inference mechanisms	Developed the free energy principle; applied predictive coding to emotion and brain functioning.
Richard Davidson	Emotion regulation, affective style, mindfulness, neuroplasticity	Demonstrated that emotional traits have neural correlates; studied the effects of meditation on brain function.
Ralph Adolphs	Social cognition, emotional processing, amygdala	Investigated the role of the amygdala in social and emotional behavior
Hugo Critchley	Interoception, autonomic function, emotional processing	Explored the neural basis of interoception and its impact on emotions

Name	Key Areas of Research	Notable Contributions
Manos Tsakiris	Interoception, body ownership, social cognition, and social and political implications of embodiment	Explored how multisensory integration underlies body ownership

for. But what if these biases are latent? Hormonally driven? Culturally supported? Culturally mandated? Do they influence the results of an experiment? These are very important questions that are definitely in play and critical for the future of the field.

It could just be one of the best ironies ever in the fields of psychology and neuroscience, if most of what we know is based on males (assumed to be cisgender) and how males experience emotions. A critical examination of the history of emotions research already reveals a systemic bias: The majority of foundational studies in neuroscience, psychology, and psychophysiology have been conducted on male subjects, both human and animal (Fletcher-Janzen et al., 2008). As a result, much of what we think we are certain about emotion and how it is experienced, regulated, and expressed is based on the neuropsychological architecture of men. Therefore, the complex influence of sex hormones, gendered socialization, and interoceptive variability in children, women, and nonbinary individuals has been historically missed, minimized, or excluded.

This bias is not accidental or unintentional; it is rooted in methodological traditions that prioritized "clean" data. Researchers often excluded females and young, particularly in animal models, because of hormonal cycles that were deemed to introduce variability. For decades, studies of fear, rage, attachment, and stress in rodent models (on which much of Jaak Panksepp's and others' neuroaffective mapping relies) were conducted almost exclusively on male rats, with assumptions that results were universally generalizable. But neuroscience now shows that this assumption is scientifically untenable (e.g. Cahill, 2006; Cosgrove et al., 2007).

Studies in humans followed similar patterns. Early research on emotion regulation, cognitive control, stress reactivity, and facial expression was largely performed on male university students (Henrich et al., 2010). Yet we know that emotional responses are shaped not only by brain structure but by hormonal modulation (e.g. estrogen, oxytocin, and progesterone), early relational experience, and sociocultural context: all of which differ by sex and gender. By failing to account for these variables, the field has constructed models of emotional development and dysfunction/pathology that reflect a male-typical baseline, often positioning female or non-male patterns as atypical or dysregulated.

This bias has clinical consequences. Diagnostic criteria for mood disorders, ADHD, Posttraumatic stress disorder, and autism spectrum conditions have been shaped by symptom presentations more common in males, leading to underdiagnosis or misdiagnosis in females. For example, women's emotion regulation strategies (e.g. internalizing, somatization, and ruminative grief) may be overlooked or pathologized because they do not fit male-centric models of expressive behavior (Jane et al., 2007). Similarly, females with high-functioning autism often go unrecognized because the emotional and social impairments they present do not align with male-modeled diagnostic heuristics (Fletcher-Janzen et al., 2008).

Even the construct of emotional intelligence, now embedded in educational and psychological discourse, arose from male-dominated corporate and military environments, shaping how emotional competence is defined and valued. Traits such as stoicism, affect suppression, and cognitive reframing are celebrated, while relational sensitivity, embodied expression, or emotional intuition (more common in females) have often been dismissed as unscientific or excessive (Smith, 2021).

It is worth noting that newer waves of affective neuroscience are actively challenging this history. Researchers such as Johnston and Olson (2015), Lisa Feldman Barrett (2017), Ruth Feldman (2012), and Lise Eliot (2009) have emphasized the need for sex aware and culturally contextualized models of emotional development. The National Institutes of Health (NIH) mandates since 2016 have required sex as a biological variable in animal and human research (Clayton & Collins, 2014). Yet, the legacy of male-centric emotional science remains deeply embedded in textbooks, treatment protocols, and public understanding. The Women's Brain Foundation (www.womensbrainproject.com/) is perhaps the best resource for those who wish to do a deep dive into current sex and gender differences in neuropsychological research.

In summary, the history of the neuroscience of emotion, as we know it, was not built on the human brain. It was built, overwhelmingly, on the male adult brain. Recognizing this fact is not about undermining previous research; it is about recontextualizing it, expanding it, and ensuring that future models of emotion are more inclusive of sex-based neurobiological variation, gendered social learning, and diverse lived experience. Only then can we begin to truly understand the richness and complexity of human emotion.

References

Adolphs, R. (2002). Recognizing emotion from facial expressions: Psychological and neurological mechanisms. *Behavioral and Cognitive Neuroscience Reviews*, 1(1), 21–62.
Barrett, L. F. (2017). *How emotions are made: The secret life of the brain*. Houghton Mifflin Harcourt.
Cahill, L. (2006). Why sex matters for neuroscience. *Nature Reviews Neuroscience*, 7(6), 477–484.
Clayton, J. A., & Collins, F. S. (2014). Policy: NIH to balance sex in cell and animal studies. *Nature*, 509(7500), 282–283. https://doi.org/10.1038/509282a
Cosgrove, K. P., Mazure, C. M., & Staley, J. K. (2007). Evolving knowledge of sex differences in brain structure, function, and chemistry. *Biological Psychiatry*, 62(8), 847–855.
Craig, A. D. (2009). How do you feel—now? The anterior insula and human awareness. *Nature Reviews Neuroscience*, 10(1), 59–70. https://doi.org/10.1038/nrn2555
Critchley, H. D., & Garfinkel, S. N. (2017). Interoception and emotion. *Current Opinion in Psychology*, 17, 7–14. https://doi.org/10.1016/j.copsyc.2017.04.020
Damasio, A. (1994). *Descartes' error: Emotion, reason, and the human brain*. G. P. Putnam's Sons.
Darwin, C. (1898). *The expression of the emotions in man and animals*. Appleton & Company.
Davidson, R. J. (1998). Affective style and affective disorders: Perspectives from affective neuroscience. *Cognition & Emotion*, 12(3), 307–330.
Ekman, P., & Friesen, W. V. (1971). Constants across cultures in the face and emotion. *Journal of Personality and Social Psychology,* 17(2), 124–129.
Eliot, L. (2009). *Pink brain, blue brain: How small differences grow into troublesome gaps—and what we can do about it*. Houghton Mifflin Harcourt.
Feldman, R. (2012). Oxytocin and social affiliation in humans. *Hormones and Behavior*, 61(3), 380–391.
Fletcher-Janzen, E., Strickland, T., & Reynolds, C. R. (2008). *Handbook of school neuropsychology*. Wiley.
Friston, K. (2010). The free-energy principle: A unified brain theory? *Nature Reviews Neuroscience,* 11(2), 127–138.
Henrich, J., Heine, S. J., & Norenzayan, A. (2010). The weirdest people in the world? *Behavioral and Brain Sciences*, 33(2–3), 61–83.
James, W. (1884). What is an emotion? *Mind*, 9(34), 188–205.
Jane, M., Ansell, E., & Agrawal, P. (2007). Gender differences in emotional expression and regulation: Implications for psychopathology. *Clinical Psychology Review*, 27(7), 882–894.
Johnston, S. M., & Olson, K. R. (2015). The neural correlates of gender and emotion: Toward a more balanced affective neuroscience. *Frontiers in Human Neuroscience*, 9, 23.
LeDoux, J. (2000). Emotion circuits in the brain. *Annual Review of Neuroscience*, 23, 155–184.
MacLean, P. D. (1990). *The triune brain in evolution: Role in paleocerebral functions*. Springer.
Moore, J. (2010). Behaviorism. *Psychological Record*, 60, 549–564.
Nussbaum, M. C. (2001). *Upheavals of thought: The intelligence of emotions*. Cambridge University Press.
Panksepp, J. (1998). *Affective neuroscience: The foundations of human and animal emotions*. Oxford University Press.
Panksepp, J., & Biven, L. (2012). *The archaeology of mind: Neuroevolutionary origins of human emotions*. W. W. Norton.
Papez, J. W. (1938). A proposed mechanism of emotion. *Archives of Neurology and Psychiatry*, 38(4), 725–743.
Russell, J. A. (1980). A circumplex model of affect. *Journal of Personality and Social Psychology*, 39(6), 1161–1178.
Schiller, D., Lowe, L., Becker, S., & Cromwell, H. (2022). *The human affectome project: Mapping emotion to brain and behavior*. Springer.

Smith, J. (2021). *The emotional code: Gender, culture, and the science of feeling*. Beacon Press.
Tsakiris, M. (2017). *The new body self: A neurobiological approach to self and social identity*. Oxford University Press.
Tsakiris, M., & De Preester, H. (Eds.). (2018). *The interoceptive mind: From homeostasis to awareness*. Oxford University Press.

Chapter 3

Affective Neurodevelopment

Most mammals are born with abilities that help them survive infancy. They may stand and walk right after birth or are born with spikes or scales (that are not easy to eat by predators). Some mammals are born in trees, underground, or other places that are hard to find. Nature provides mechanisms to keep the baby mammal alive. The babies' parents are built to have parenting instincts that keep the baby alive too. No one teaches a mother cat to prepare a nest for her babies, or clean them after birth, or feed them. These caregiving behaviors are on automatic pilot dictated by nature and the specifics of the environmental conditions of a species.

Human babies, on the other hand, have no protections built in at birth. They are totally dependent on caregivers for staying alive. They cannot move much, feed themselves, regulate their body temperature, or defend themselves against any predators. So how has nature provided for human babies? How do we stay alive? The answer is biological and instinctual: attachment.

An interesting fact that provides the key to human attachment is the fact that within ten minutes of being born, babies prefer to look at faces rather than anything else (shapes etc.) (Goren et al., 1975). The human baby brain has the built in instinct (via an area of the brain called the fusiform gyrus or "face recognition area") to be attracted to human faces. The overall eyes, nose, and mouth configuration is irresistible to a baby. Why? Well, it makes sense that if human babies need total caregiving to stay alive, they must create a relationship with the caregivers that are around otherwise care could be random or negligent and seriously impede survival. It is therefore very important for humans to recognize the faces of those who take care of us. There must be an emotional feeling of safety and attraction to our caregivers. Bonding implies that it is a two-way street because the caregiver has to be bonded to the infant as well. In fact, the caregiver must be compelled to stay with the infant to the point where it is painful or scary to be away from the child. If human caregivers were not instinctually designed to bond with infants, then abandonment would be easy, and this is not good for the survival of the human species. So, the love affair begins with the baby orienting toward the caregiver's face and being primed by nature to have high levels of a hormone called oxytocin in the body system.

Usually nicknamed the "love or cuddle" hormone, oxytocin creates feelings of social trust, care, love, warmth, and connection (more on this hormone in Chapter 10). This hormone is also connected with milk let-down, so nature links faces, feeding, and cuddling with safety and survival. This is the instinctual and biological basis of human attachment and the basis for the development of emotions.

DOI: 10.4324/9781003745686-4

Human babies communicate in pretty basic ways. If they like something they show it immediately by smiling, cooing, snuggling, and reaching out for more. If they do not like something they cry, scream, yell, and push away. These behaviors are basic approach or avoidance mannerisms that get the attention of the caregivers who will adjust the environment to suit what the baby wants. The valence of positive and negative, or approach avoidance is very easy to see in babies. They act out their thoughts and feelings so we can see what is going on with them and help them out. They act out their emotions of love, play, sadness, fear, anger, and curiosity because the front part of the brain responsible for decision-making, the language centers of the brain, and physical coordination are too underdeveloped to be expressed independently. Therefore, emotions, in infancy, are very instinctual, nonverbal, and physical. They tend to be whole body experiences and oriented for general positive or negative feelings. There are two types of emotions at this stage: homeostatic emotions (hunger, pain, temperature etc.) and social emotions such as rage, care, play, seeking, sadness, and fear (Craig, 2010). Regardless of the type, it is important to remember that in human development emotions precede language. In fact, emotions are the way that baby humans communicate and operate on the world.

Social Context and Brain Growth

You may recognize that this delightful and preverbal cuddly attachment dictated by nature also only takes place in a social context. That right from the beginning, the social relationship is what keeps the baby alive, and the continued unfolding of the relationship cements the child's very future. How so? If we look at what happens when the social relationship is not there for some groups of children (e.g. institutionalized orphans where there is very large caregiver to child ratios) we start to see how important social air actually is for brain development (Wiik et al., 2011). Much of the research literature on early deprivation shows that children who are deprived of social interaction do not thrive. In fact, with severe deprivation, the child dies or sustains significant brain alterations that create severe pathology. Love, touch, cuddles, giggles, eye contact, responsiveness to crying etc. are essential activities that literally grow the baby's brain (Kolb et al., 2017). Neuronal growth is abundant and exponential during normal attachment and attunement. Deprivation alters the course of brain development, and you will see institutionalized and neglected babies rocking, staring, listless, and depressed. A reversal of this process can happen if the child is adopted into a loving and caring environment, however, it is too often the case that these children start to show a marked lacking in empathy later on in childhood (Fries et al., 2004).

Empathy is the bedrock of many emotions, and it is the glue that cements relationships and a sense of self. When caregivers and children are attached and attuned to each other, over the course of time they can predict what each other needs and how to deliver. In this way, emotions become the essence of empathy, of social relationships, and the ability to predict and course correct our thoughts/cognitions. They are the wellspring of how we get what we want in life. It is social air, and it is essential to breathe it if we are to survive.

Communication of Emotions Across Development

When we are past infancy and early childhood, these whole-body emotional instincts still determine how we feel at any given time during the day. However, once language has become developed to the point where we can orally describe an emotional source, then we are expected to translate the approach/avoidance into clear thoughts about what we want or what we are experiencing.

Just because we have more mature rational thinking and language capabilities when we grow into adolescence and adulthood, does not mean that the instinctual and embodied emotions that we felt in early childhood are not present. They are. What has changed is that we do not need to rely on our caregivers to approach or avoid things for us in the environment anymore, we can do that ourselves with verbal and nonverbal expression. Herein lies the rub: just because we can intellectualize and verbalize our basic emotions quickly does not mean that we should. In fact, research (e.g. Lieberman et al., 2007) indicates that when we sense an approach/avoidance situation it is best if we sit with our basic instinctual emotions so that we can use them to identify and realize a goal. For example, if something we see is negative and it makes us angry then we need to be fully aware that this emotion is telling us something very important: that we must protect something of import to us. If the goal is to protect, then our intellectual parts of our brains can quickly and easily come up with great strategies to protect. However, if we think that feeling angry is a bad thing, then we will repress this body experience and tend to stay up in the frontal lobes and "rational" part of the brain trying to figure out exactly what we need to do. Once we start thinking (without recognizing the underlying emotion) we start going down rabbit holes and may well not get what we want or need. What if something makes you angry and you were trained to say to yourself "oh, it's not ok to feel angry, I will ignore it" and you do literally ignore it, how will you protect yourself? On the other hand, sometimes you will need to suppress anger because it is more dangerous to express it. Hopefully the latter is consciously done, otherwise the underlying and unacknowledged anger may seep out in unintended ways.

Once language has been internalized in childhood, we have inner speech and thought becomes language (Vygotsky, 1978). Depending on what is taught to us by our culture at that time, our inner speech becomes our consciousness and our sense of self (or default mode network in neuroscientific terms; Raichle et al., 2001). Our sense of self is dependent on what we like to approach and what we tend to avoid and much of that valence is taught to us by our caregivers. Therefore, the expression of our inner experiences with emotions is very much culturally and environmentally driven.

It is said that each language has its own set of favorite words for emotions. In some cultures, there are no words for one type of emotion but multiple words for other types of emotions. So, we do not have a panhuman set of descriptors for each of the seven basic emotions. In fact, the words that we use for these emotions in this book are limited by the English language and western first-world culture. Jaak Panksepp's RAGE, PANIC-GRIEF, PLAY, LUST, CARE, SEEKING, FEAR are English words that may play out differently in non-English-speaking cultures. These words also do not have tight definitions because all emotions are expressed on a continuum from mild to intense. Therefore, we can be a bit annoyed, or we can be incensed; or disappointed or bereft of hope; or amused or ecstatic. Emotions are really moving targets that are contextually and culturally molded. One aspect about emotions, however, is consistent: We all have the seven basic biological (homeostatic and allostatic) set of emotional tools regardless of where we are born or how we are raised. We all have the biological wiring for emotions, and the wiring is expressed dynamically almost all of the time.

Embodied Cognition

One of the most sophisticated (and difficult) things for a human to do is to use language to describe what emotions we are feeling. It is a higher order activity and sometimes words escape the best of us when experiencing a complex set of emotions. Paradoxically, we use emotions (homeostatic and social) in our communications all the time (Eagleman, 2020). We find a person "warm", we need to "cool off" when agitated, or someone says that they're speaking with a "heavy heart". It is interesting to start looking out for these embodied terms and usually the more you identify the easier it is to locate them.

Studies have shown that understanding action-related words (like "kick" or "grab") activates the same brain regions involved in performing those actions. Gestures, too, are an integral part of communication and can influence thought processes. Research shows that perception is not just about passively receiving information from the environment but is also shaped by our bodily capabilities and actions (Eagleman, 2020; Pulvermüller et al., 2005). For instance, how we perceive the size of an object can change based on our ability to interact with it, such as heavy files are considered to contain more important information than those that are light in weight. In addition, adopting certain postures can affect a person's mood or confidence levels, and facial expressions can certainly impact how emotions are felt (Eagleman, 2020; Veenstra, 2017).

Therefore, embodied cognition extends the idea of cognitive processes beyond the brain to include the entire body and its interaction with the world. This includes the concept of "extended cognition", where tools and external objects become part of the cognitive process (e.g. using a calculator or AI as an extension of one's cognitive abilities). Emotions are physically embodied and linguistically involved in everything we do because emotions are our first thoughts, and we communicate them through the body to streamline the social air that we breathe. Embodied cognition research has reshaped our understanding of the mind by highlighting the critical role of the body in cognitive processes, challenging traditional views that separated the mind from the physical world.

Nonverbal Expression of Emotion

We also do not have to use words to convey emotions to another human. We have to be aware that humans show our emotions on our faces and with nonverbal actions. Nature provides us with a specific part of the brain that is used primarily for recognizing faces. Not only does this area allow for us to recognize our caregivers face in infancy, but it also allows an almost instant recognition of how another is feeling. Facial expressions are important for survival because we need to communicate fast in dangerous situations, for example, you are talking to someone and they look over your shoulder and their facial expression changes to mouth open, eyes wide or grimace, what do you think? What do you do? On the other hand, you might see a smile that imparts safety, and it can make your parasympathetic nervous system relax and your body feel safe. So much information in a facial expression and how efficient! In terms of homeostasis and allostasis, we humans cannot wait around to hear all the words that someone might use to let us know how they are feeling, we need augmentation with nonverbal signs that are quick and powerful so we can react appropriately.

In the end, we have the flexibility of being able to translate emotions in a flash of a second or take our time and verbally tell a narrative about what we are feeling. It takes both to be well adjusted and meet life's demands. This flexibility is also the essence of social air. We sail through our social-emotional lives juggling so many different sensations, words, and physical expressions and the bigger the repertoire of skills the better!

Together, these ideas remind us that human emotional life begins long before words and is rooted in biology, shaped through relationships, and carried forward by culture and experience. From the newborn's instinctive search for a caregiver's face to the adolescent's internal dialogue about what emotions mean, our feelings are both embodied and social. They help us read the world, protect what matters, and connect with others. When early relationships are nurturing, emotions become reliable tools for navigating life; when they are disrupted, the emotional landscape becomes harder to interpret and trust. Across development, we weave together instinct, language, culture, and bodily cues to form a sense of self that can respond flexibly to life's challenges. This ongoing dance between body, brain, and environment is the foundation of emotional intelligence and the heart of what it means to be human.

References

Craig, A. D. (2010). The sentient self. *Brain Structure and Function*, 214(5–6), 563–577. https://doi.org/10.1007/s00429-010-0248-y
Eagleman, D. (2020). *Livewired: The inside story of the ever-changing brain*. Pantheon Books.
Fries, A. B. W., Ziegler, T. E., Kurian, J. R., Jacoris, S., & Pollak, S. D. (2004). Early experience in humans is associated with changes in neuropeptides critical for regulating social behavior. *Proceedings of the National Academy of Sciences*, 102(47), 17237–17240.
Goren, C. C., Sarty, M., & Wu, P. Y. K. (1975). Visual following and pattern discrimination of face-like stimuli by newborn infants. *Pediatrics*, 56(4), 544–549.
Kolb, B., Harker, A., & Gibb, R. (2017). Principles of plasticity in the developing brain. *Developmental Medicine & Child Neurology*, 59(12), 1218–1223.
Lieberman, M. D., Eisenberger, N. I., Crockett, M. J., Tom, S. M., Pfeifer, J. H., & Way, B. M. (2007). Putting feelings into words: Affect labeling disrupts amygdala activity in response to affective stimuli. *Psychological Science*, 18(5), 421–428.
Pulvermüller, F., Hauk, O., Nikulin, V. V., & Ilmoniemi, R. J. (2005). Functional links between motor and language systems. *European Journal of Neuroscience*, 21(3), 793–797.
Raichle, M. E., MacLeod, A. M., Snyder, A. Z., Powers, W. J., Gusnard, D. A., & Shulman, G. L. (2001). A default mode of brain function. *Proceedings of the National Academy of Sciences*, 98(2), 676–682.
Veenstra, L. (2017). Facial feedback and emotion: Revisiting the facial feedback hypothesis. *Cognition and Emotion*, 31(8), 1558–1572.
Vygotsky, L. S. (1978). *Mind in society: The development of higher psychological processes*. Harvard University Press.
Wiik, K. L., Loman, M. M., Van Ryzin, M. J., Armstrong, J. M., Essex, M. J., Pollak, S. D., & Gunnar, M. R. (2011). Behavioral and emotional symptoms of post-institutionalized children in middle childhood. *Journal of Child Psychology and Psychiatry*, 52(1), 56–63.

Chapter 4

The Paradigm Shift

How Do We Feel?

Affective neuroscience has transformed the understanding of emotions, from being dismissed as irrational impulses, to recognizing them as biologically rooted processes that arise in the body to support homeostasis and guide adaptive behavior through allostasis.

Top-Down and Bottom-Up Emotional Processing

This is also a good place to define what we mean by top-down and bottom-up brain processing. It is important to know the difference because we have to choose where to start when we want to educate and intervene with individuals about emotions. Do we start with cognitive talk therapies? (top) Or do we start with somatic inventories that ask "how does that feel in your body?" (bottom). When we say top-down/bottom-up we mean it literally!

Top-down processing refers to how the brain uses prior knowledge, experiences, expectations, and goals to interpret and influence incoming sensory information. These processes are usually associated with frontal and upper regions of the brain. Rather than simply reacting to stimuli, the brain actively predicts and shapes perception by sending signals from higher-order cognitive areas (like the prefrontal cortex) down to lower-level sensory regions. This process helps us: quickly make sense of ambiguous or incomplete information, focus attention on what is relevant, and interpret the world based on context and memory. In essence, top-down processing reflects the brain's interpretive and anticipatory role. It does not just receive input, it actively constructs perception based on what it already knows (Engle et al., 2001).

Bottom-up processing, on the other hand, is all about how we build our perception of the world starting from the ground up literally from our senses. It begins when something in the inside or outside our bodies stimulates our eyes, ears, skin, or other sensory systems. That raw data (light, sound waves, textures, primal emotions, and interoceptive messages) get passed upward into the brain, where it is gradually assembled into something meaningful. This process is reactive and immediate. The brain isn't guessing or interpreting yet; it's simply receiving, step by step, constructing perception based on what is being felt. In essence, bottom-up processing reflects how external stimuli enter the system, travel through lower-level sensory pathways, and then is processed into conscious experience. The moment it becomes conscious, then the whole brain is working with the information (Engle et al., 2001; Pessoa & Adolphs, 2010).

DOI: 10.4324/9781003745686-5

This brings us back to interoception. In a world that culturally values top-down dominance and the discounting of basic internal perceptions, (I think therefore I am) we tend to omit teaching children to honor and understand their internal experiences and err on the side of compliance as opposed to agency (Mahler, 2015). Interoception upends this thinking and leads us back to our bodies.

Interoception: The Sense of the Body's Interior

If there was going to be only one line of research that has shifted the way we think about emotions and affective neuroscience, it would be that focused on interoception. Interoception refers to the sense of the internal state of the body. It involves the brain's ability to perceive, interpret, and integrate signals originating from inside the body, such as heart rate, respiration, hunger, thirst, and the sensation of internal organs. This process is crucial for maintaining homeostasis and allostasis and plays a significant role in emotional experiences, decision-making, and overall well-being (e.g. Craig, 2009; 2010; Tsakiris & De Preester, 2018).

We need to look to the life-long work of an exceptional neuroscientist, A. D. (Bud) Craig (2009; 2010), to understand the importance of the role of interoception in emotional functioning. He identified the insular cortex as a critical brain region for processing interoceptive signals, such as temperature, pain, and the physiological condition of internal organs and how the insula integrates these signals to contribute to our conscious awareness of what we are feeling. Craig suggested that the anterior insula plays a key role in integrating interoceptive information with emotional and cognitive processes. Craig's research also involved detailed neuroanatomical mapping, tracing the pathways that interoceptive signals take from the body to the brain, and how they are interpreted to related to homeostatic needs. He conducted extensive research on how the brain perceives temperature and pain, mapping the pathways through which these sensations are transmitted from the body to the brain. His work helped clarify how these sensory experiences contribute to emotional states and debunked the traditional view that sensory experiences only went to the sensory cortex of the brain. The later supported a dualistic view of separating the brain and body whereas Craig's work showed how they meld at all times. Craig also found that the pathways for pain in the body are also involved in the pain of social isolation.

The whole line of research on interoception led and cemented by Craig, has provided the backbone of understanding the mind/brain–body connection and this base has created a new area of practical applications for occupational therapy (Mahler, 2015) and counseling by supporting clients exploring the sensory as well as the cognitive aspects of their issues.

Craig is joined by many other researchers who emphasize the role of bottom-up brain structures in generating emotional experience. These subcortical systems detect changes in internal states (like hunger, pain, or arousal) and external environmental cues (like threat, novelty, or social signals) and translate them into affective responses that prepare the body for action.

This bottom-up process begins with interoceptive and sensory input. The brain continuously monitors signals from the body such as heart rate, respiration, gut tension, and hormonal shifts via the vagus nerve, spinal cord, and lamina I neurons of the spinal dorsal horn. These signals travel to the brainstem and then to the posterior insula, where they are integrated into a "map" of the body's physiological state. When a significant shift occurs, such as a drop in blood sugar or the presence of danger, this information is automatically flagged and passed forward through limbic circuits, particularly the amygdala, hypothalamus, and anterior cingulate cortex, which initiate autonomic, hormonal, and behavioral responses. All of this occurs before the prefrontal cortex is even involved (Craig, 2009).

In other words, we feel before we think. The conscious awareness of an emotion, or the labeling of it as "sadness", "anger", or "fear", is a top-down interpretation of this initial bottom-up wave of sensation, arousal, and action preparation. The prefrontal cortex, especially the ventromedial and orbitofrontal regions, helps regulate, contextualize, and reflect on these emotional signals, but it does not create them. In young children, whose prefrontal systems are still developing, this explains why emotional reactions are often intense, physical, and poorly regulated. They are experiencing affective states from the bottom up, with minimal top-down modulation.

Understanding emotions as bottom-up processes allows clinicians to appreciate why cognitive strategies alone are often insufficient for emotional regulation, especially in children or individuals with trauma. Cognitive strategies like reframing, positive self-talk, or problem-solving are often the tools we reach for when trying to help children regulate their emotions. But for many individuals, especially children and those with histories of trauma, these top-down approaches may easily misinterpret the emotional confusion that is trying to be expressed. And it is not a matter of motivation or effort: It is a matter of neurodevelopment and neurobiology.

In young children, the prefrontal cortex, the part of the brain responsible for impulse control, flexible thinking, and emotional modulation is still developing. These cortical systems mature gradually across childhood and adolescence, and they are among the last regions of the brain to fully wire (Kolb & Whishaw, 2015). This means children do not yet have the internal architecture to regulate intense feelings through thought alone. Their capacity for self-regulation depends heavily on external support, predictable environments, and the presence of safe, attuned adults.

For individuals who have experienced trauma, the situation becomes even more complex. Chronic stress and early adversity disrupt the balance between the limbic system and the prefrontal cortex. In particular, trauma can lead to heightened activity in the amygdala, the brain's threat detector, and reduced connectivity to the prefrontal areas that help inhibit emotional reactivity (Perry, 2001). In these moments, the brain shifts into a state of survival. It prioritizes immediate protection over reflection or logic. The thinking brain goes offline. Trying to engage in cognitive strategies under these conditions is like trying to apply the brakes on a car that has already flown off the road.

Emotions originate from the bottom up. They begin in the body, in sensations that arise from the viscera, the muscles, and the autonomic nervous system. These sensations travel through the spinal cord and brainstem, up to the limbic system, where they are appraised for urgency and salience. The thinking brain only comes online after the emotional brain has already begun to respond. If the body is dysregulated (tense, flooded, or immobilized) there is simply little access to cognitive tools. This is not a weakness. It is a biologically adaptive pattern designed to protect the organism.

That is why bottom-up regulation must come first in treatment. For children and trauma survivors, regulation often begins in relationships and through co-regulation. The presence of a calm, steady caregiver who offers rhythm, warmth, and safety can help shift the nervous system back into balance. Once the brain feels safe, the prefrontal cortex begins to re-engage. Only then do cognitive strategies become useful.

In practice, this means that helping a child calm down does not start with reasoning or lectures. It starts with breath, with rhythm, with tone, with proximity. It starts by regulating the body, not correcting the behavior. And in doing so, we build the foundation for lasting emotional resilience not through words alone, but through safety felt in the body.

Regulation must begin with body-based approaches such as co-regulation, sensory input, breathing, movement, or safe relational presence to calm the foundational circuits before cognitive reflection becomes possible. Emotional healing, therefore, often starts not with insight, but with safety, sensory grounding, and attunement to bodily states.

Defining Emotions from an Affective Neuroscience Perspective: The Paradigm Shift

The Oxford English Dictionary (2025) suggests the word "emotion" is borrowed from French and English. In French, emouvoir means to "excite" or "to move out, remove, stir up, or agitate". The Latin word, emovere, is from 3- (variant of ex-) "out" + movere "move". These linguistic bases are so very appropriate as they adequately reflect how current affective neuroscience views the practical uses of emotions: They are ways of moving through the world. They are survival guides for humans navigating a complex world (Montag & Panksepp, 2017) and are considered biological ancestral voices. Emotions are genetically and evolutionarily endowed core affective states that are not learned, they are biologically prewired. However, they are most definitely agents that adapt and learn through memory and experience and morph in millions of ways to meet internal and environmental demands.

There are some operative words in the last paragraph that might explain the paradigm shift that affective neuroscience seeks to present. The assumption that we should be feeling good all the time and that negative emotions derail us is simply incorrect. Our number one goal is not to feel good; it is to *survive*. All our biological, psychological, and social needs serve our continued existence, and our existence is dependent on our skill sets for allostasis.

Allostasis: Surviving and Thriving

What is allostasis? We are all familiar with the term homeostasis. It basically describes how an organism (including humans) keeps certain bodily demands/functions within a certain tolerance so that the organism survives. Allostasis extends homeostasis by looking at how flexible an organism can be when it juggles internal and external demands, so it not just survives biologically but *thrives* (Sterling, 1988). We humans, to win our lifetime race, need to be adept at allostasis because our lives are not just about simple temperature control, intake of food, hydration etc. We are in the human race, and it involves having a great support system, careers, making money, mortgages, soccer games and a myriad of other human pursuits. For these multiple pursuits we need a big toolbox so we can be strong enough to hold to our values and yet flexible enough to pivot at a moment's notice. The image of a willow tree is appropriate for this idea: A willow tree is strong enough to hold back the banks of a river and yet flexible enough to make shelter, baskets, and weaved fences. We humans must be willows if we are to survive *and* thrive and emotions are the tools that give us what we need to do just that.

It might be good to spend a little time with "allostasis" because it is central to the affective neuroscientific shift on emotions. Allostasis a concept in physiology and neuroscience that describes how the body maintains stability through change (Sterling, 1988). Unlike homeostasis, which refers to the maintenance of a stable internal environment, allostasis focuses on how the body proactively adjusts to anticipated stressors and demands, using various physiological systems to achieve stability. Without a central hub for management, maintaining the body is quite difficult. At its base, allostasis allows the brain and body to manage energy resources efficiently and to respond to threats to homeostasis preferably *before* they occur. The operative idea for allostasis to work well then is "prediction" (Sterling, 2012). The brain needs to predict and coordinate bodily changes and responses to maximize homeostasis. It also needs to realize when there are prediction errors and adjust accordingly. But we are not just talking about the management of the biological systems in homeostasis here. We are also including emotions. There are homeostatic emotions (as mentioned before, temperature, hunger, thirst etc.) but there also social emotions such as anger, care, and play. These instinctual drives are also in the body and are needed for survival. When life's emotions, both homeostatic and social, become overwhelmed on a chronic basis we then encounter allostatic load and this is defined as a cumulative result of repeated or chronic stress (Sterling, 1988). When allostatic overload and gene expression come together, we see poor immune functioning and the resultant chronic diseases associated with prolonged stress. A good basic way to think about emotions is that they are tools that help us maintain being physically alive (homeostasis) and tools that help us navigate the social world that we live in so we can survive and thrive (allostasis) (Sterling, 2020).

Translating the Paradigm Shift into Practice

It should be remembered that while the new field of affective neuroscience defines emotions as dynamic bottom-up *and* top-down tools for allostatic living, mainstream psychology defines emotions in a more ambiguous way as "conscious mental reactions (such as anger or fear) subjectively experienced as strong feelings usually directed toward a specific object and typically accompanied by physiological and behavioral changes in the body" (APA, 2025). This is still essentially a top-down approach even though the body is mentioned in the definition. Some take this top-down reductionist position to propose that we totally construct our emotions from our social world and that we do not possess core brain–body wiring for different affective states. This is doubling down on the idea that emotions are created in the upper regions of the brain first. Indeed, they can be but not at the expense of ignoring the body's contribution. To ignore the body is to ignore our ancestors and the self. To ignore the self is to dismantle agency. The problem with any extreme point of view is that it is not practical or flexible. By ignoring the body–brain connection (often through the gut but that is another conversation…), we deny the power of the body to influence the regulation of homeostasis and allostasis: Why would we want to do that? Why would we want to abandon what our bodies are telling us about survival to listen to an interpretation of what we "think" might be going on?

In the end, it is not about either or. There are times when the brain should influence the body and times when the body should influence the brain. Together they are a great team, and when working together, the brain–body makes really good choices! (Futos et al., 2013). The issue at hand, is that mainstream psychology still adheres to "I think therefore I am" where total cognitive control over everything we do is lauded as a virtue and a desirable mental goal. Hence, we see terms about emotion that emphasize cognitive control such as "emotional control", "emotional regulation", and "emotional intelligence". We see subtle and implicit labels that create expectations in us to always be rational, to be cerebral, to suppress our deepest energy (and the heart of our quest for survival?). Somehow, somewhere along the way, we have formed rules about emotions being irrational and if you display emotions, you must vulnerable and weak and incapable of making good decisions. This is simply not true. In fact, research about the human affectome is well on its way to suggesting the opposite.

This paradigm shift is about how we think about the basic premise of human agency. Let me say this again, because it is very important for all of us to value the brain–body approach, but it is absolutely critical to use this perspective for groups or individuals who have been marginalized by society. It is difficult for marginalized groups to feel like they have agency to change their lives if mainstream culture is dominating the cultural value of the deepest parts of what it is to be human. Mainstream society (and psychological sciences) tends to want humans to be under tight control so that behaviors are not culturally disruptive. It is about compliance to the norm. The underlying assumption is that showing emotion is weak, not civilized, or shows lack of mental discipline. There seems to be no distinction between having an emotion and being hysterical or violent! Affective neuroscience, on the other hand, is showing that being aware of a deep emotion actually enhances the individual's ability to develop efficient use of energy and manage their world. What you feel does not impel you to act irrationally, it impels you to act, period. If you do not know what you feel, then predicting a path forward is prone to error and boundaries are lost. The theme of this book is to help clients bring the body back into harmony with the brain as we are biologically meant to do. The goal is to maximize the usefulness of sensory information that comes in, meld it with past experience, and understand the way forward.

References

American Psychological Association. (2025). *APA dictionary of psychology* (3rd ed.). American Psychological Association.

Craig, A. D. (2009). How do you feel—now? The anterior insula and human awareness. *Nature Reviews Neuroscience*, 10(1), 59–70. https://doi.org/10.1038/nrn2555

Craig, A. D. (2010). The sentient self. *Brain Structure and Function*, 214(5–6), 563–577. https://doi.org/10.1007/s00429-010-0248-y

Engle, A. K., Fries, P., & Singer, W. (2001). Dynamic predictions: Oscillations and synchrony in top–down processing. *Nature Reviews Neuroscience*, 2(10), 704–716.

Futos, J., Panksepp, J., & Davis, K. L. (2013). *The affective neuroscience of consciousness: Core emotional systems and implications for understanding the human mind*. Springer.

Kolb, B., & Whishaw, I. Q. (2015). *An introduction to brain and behavior* (4th ed.). Worth Publishers.

Mahler, K. J. (2015). *Interoception: The eighth sensory system*. AAPC Publishing.

Montag, C., & Panksepp, J. (2017). Primary emotional systems and personality: An evolutionary perspective. *Frontiers in Psychology*, 8, 464. https://doi.org/10.3389/fpsyg.2017.00464

Perry, B. D. (2001). The neurodevelopmental impact of violence in childhood. In D. Schetky & E. P. Benedek (Eds.), *Textbook of child and adolescent forensic psychiatry* (pp. 221–238). American Psychiatric Press.

Pessoa, L., & Adolphs, R. (2010). Emotion processing and the amygdala: From a 'low road' to 'many roads' of evaluating biological significance. *Nature Reviews Neuroscience*, 11(11), 773–783.

Sterling, P. (1988). Allostasis: A model of predictive regulation. In G. M. Sterling (Ed.), *Handbook of physiology: Section 7, The nervous system* (Vol. 2, pp. 625–637). American Physiological Society.

Sterling, P. (2012). Allostasis: A model of predictive regulation. *Physiology & Behavior*, 106(1), 5–15.

Sterling, P. (2020). *What is health? Allostasis and the evolution of human design*. MIT Press.

Tsakiris, M., & De Preester, H. (Eds.). (2018). *The interoceptive mind: From homeostasis to awareness*. Oxford University Press.

Chapter 5

Essential Research on Affective Neuroscience

This is a heavyweight chapter that hopefully codifies where affective neuroscience is at the moment. It summarizes the research base and the main actors in the field whose research have created a substantial body of knowledge that is manifesting and sustaining a paradigm shift. It has been incorporated here for multiple reasons. The Affective Inventory, that is later described in the book, brings this research to life in the therapy room. This section also provides the curious reader with more information on outstanding lines of thought that are rapidly converging.

In science and practice, we build on the foundations laid by those who came before us. While detailed reviews of individual studies are valuable, they are beyond the scope of this book. Instead, the focus will remain on the overarching ideas that signal a broader paradigm shift in how we understand emotion and the brain–body connection. This chapter, then, takes an annotative bibliographic approach, highlighting key contributions from prominent researchers whose work has shaped and consolidated the field of affective neuroscience.

Jaak Panksepp

Jaak Panksepp's (e.g. 1998; 2012) work is central to the current field of emotions research and is the central basis for this book. Therefore, it is appropriate for us to spend quite a bit of time delving into his seminal work. Over the span of five decades, Panksepp carved out a space for the scientific study of emotions, not as abstractions or behavioral byproducts, but as deeply embedded neural systems that guide the lives of mammals, including humans. He called this field Affective Neuroscience, and his contributions to it are both foundational and enduring.

What made Panksepp unique was his willingness to go deep, literally, into the subcortical brain. At a time when cognitive science was focused on thoughts, language, and high-level cortical functions, he was exploring the midbrain and brainstem, using electrical stimulation and lesion studies to map emotional circuits in animals. His findings pointed to seven primary-process emotional systems: SEEKING, CARE, PLAY, and LUST as positive, exploratory, and affiliative drives; and FEAR, RAGE, and PANIC as ancient survival mechanisms tied to danger, frustration, and separation distress.

Each of these systems was linked to specific neural pathways and neurochemical signatures. And crucially, each generated subjective feeling states. That is, perhaps, the most radical aspect

DOI: 10.4324/9781003745686-6

of Panksepp's work: He argued that animals do not merely behave as if they feel, they actually feel. Their cries of separation, their play calls, their startled freezing are not just reactions, but signs of interior emotional life. For Panksepp, affect wasn't secondary to cognition: It was the foundation upon which cognitive processes are built.

This bottom-up view of emotion helped reframe psychiatric disorders. Depression, for instance, could be understood as a dysregulation of the PANIC and SEEKING systems. Addiction might involve hijacking of the SEEKING circuitry by substances that mimic internal rewards. Treatments, then, might be more effective if they targeted these deep, ancient emotional networks. He proposed, and in some cases helped to test, novel therapies such as deep brain stimulation of the SEEKING system for treatment-resistant depression and low-dose naltrexone for autism spectrum disorders, based on his opioid hypothesis of social pain.

In the final years of his career, Panksepp found himself both celebrated and contested. He challenged dominant models that framed emotion as a cortical construct or a cognitively generated "readout". Instead, he held firm to the view that feeling emerges first from our subcortical architecture and is later interpreted, modulated, and shaped by the cortex. That position still stirs debate, but it also opens the door to a fuller understanding of consciousness, one that starts not with language or rationality, but with sensation and need. In the end, Panksepp's legacy is not only in his research findings but in his insistence that emotion matters not just behaviorally or cognitively, but experientially. He reminded us that to be alive is to feel, and that those feelings are not peripheral to the human condition because they are its core.

Panksepp's book, the *Archaeology of Mind* (Panksepp & Biven, 2012) is a seminal book that encapsulates his research and findings. It is a detailed anthology of his work and written in a practical manner that is well worth the effort of study. The breadth and depth of the book is vast and so it may take the reader some time to digest. However, fundamental shifts in the way we think about emotions are not easy or small and Panksepp's work is well worth the time needed for deep thinking and shifts. His book is more of a journey (intellectually, emotionally, professionally, and personally) than a lesson or class. The book is also a way for you to start a bottom-up mapping of the mammalian brain that will help you know where to start your interventions. Some interventions need a top-down approach, and others must go from bottom-up otherwise therapy goals will not hit the mark. Panksepp's work illuminates the lower and lesser-known systems in the brain that influence the upper regions where conscious decisions, choices, movements, and actions are made.

Panksepp's Seven Core Emotional Systems

The seven core emotional systems represent deep, evolutionarily conserved circuits in the mammalian brain. These systems are not mere abstractions, they are living, breathing patterns of neural activity that shape how we feel, connect, and survive. They arise from subcortical (nonconscious or subconscious) structures and are closely tied to basic survival functions, while also scaffolding complex human behaviors and social bonds. What follows is a brief (note that detailed descriptions are presented in Chapters 6 through 12) narrative integration of their function, core brain regions, associated neurochemicals, and their anatomical substrates outlined by Panksepp (1998) and Panksepp & Biven (2012). Table 5.1 shows these aspects in table format for easy reference.

Seeking

The SEEKING system is the engine of exploration, curiosity, and purposeful engagement with the world. Centered in the ventral tegmental area and extending through the nucleus accumbens to the medial prefrontal cortex, this system is fueled by dopamine. It urges the organism to

Table 5.1 Panksepp's Seven Core Emotional Systems with Neuroanatomical Locations

Panksepp Core Emotional System	Function	Key Brain Regions	Neurochemicals	Neuroanatomical Locations
SEEKING	Generates curiosity, motivation, anticipation, and goal-directed behavior; promotes learning and exploration	Ventral tegmental area (VTA), nucleus accumbens (NAc), medial forebrain bundle, lateral hypothalamus	Dopamine, glutamate, endogenous opioids	Mesolimbic dopamine system; midbrain to forebrain projections
RAGE	Facilitates defensive aggression and protest; activated by frustration or restraint	Medial amygdala, hypothalamus (medial), periaqueductal gray (PAG)	Substance P, glutamate, testosterone, CRF	Medial hypothalamus and PAG in midbrain
FEAR	Triggers escape, freezing, or defensive behaviors in response to threats	Amygdala, hypothalamus, PAG, bed nucleus of the stria terminalis (BNST)	Glutamate, CRF, GABA, norepinephrine	Amygdala-centered circuit; projections to PAG and hypothalamus
LUST	Drives sexual behavior and reproductive motivation	Medial preoptic area (MPOA), ventromedial hypothalamus (VMH), nucleus accumbens	Estrogen, testosterone, dopamine, oxytocin	MPOA of hypothalamus; mesolimbic structures

(*Continued*)

Panksepp Core Emotional System	Function	Key Brain Regions	Neurochemicals	Neuroanatomical Locations
CARE	Supports nurturing, bonding, and affectionate behaviors; essential for attachment and caregiving	Anterior cingulate cortex, preoptic area, BNST	Oxytocin, prolactin, endogenous opioids	Hypothalamus (MPOA and BNST); anterior cingulate cortex
PANIC/ GRIEF	Triggers crying, protest, and social separation anxiety; promotes reunion and social bonding	Dorsal anterior cingulate cortex (dACC), PAG, thalamus	Endogenous opioids, CRF, oxytocin	Cingulate cortex, dorsomedial thalamus, dorsal PAG
PLAY	Promotes social joy, learning social rules, and development of social competence	Parafascicular thalamus, dorsomedial diencephalon, frontal cortex	Dopamine, endogenous opioids, IGF-1 (likely)	Subcortical-cortical circuits including thalamus and frontal cortex

investigate its environment, pursue goals, and anticipate rewards. Anatomically, it spans the midbrain and projects forward into limbic and cortical regions, forming a mesolimbic-mesocortical network that underlies motivation and learning.

Rage

RAGE is a reactive, mobilizing system that prepares the body to confront threats or obstacles. When an animal is restrained or provoked, circuits linking the medial amygdala, hypothalamus, and periaqueductal gray activate. This system is powered by substances like Substance P and glutamate, facilitating intense emotional arousal. It arises in the diencephalon and midbrain, enabling quick, defensive responses vital for survival.

Fear

The FEAR system orchestrates escape and avoidance in the face of danger. Its epicenter lies in the amygdala, which communicates with the hypothalamus and periaqueductal gray to coordinate freezing or fleeing behaviors. Neurochemicals such as corticotropin-releasing factor (CRF), glutamate, and norepinephrine heighten vigilance. Neuroanatomically, it is anchored in the amygdaloid complex and radiates into lower brain regions to swiftly activate survival responses.

Lust

LUST governs sexual arousal and reproductive behaviors. Deep in the hypothalamus, the medial preoptic area and the ventromedial nucleus regulate mating instincts, mediated by testosterone, estrogen, oxytocin, and vasopressin. These hormones modulate attraction and bonding, anchoring LUST in evolutionary imperatives. This circuitry is embedded in hypothalamic and limbic networks that shape intimacy and LUST.

Care

The CARE system is the neurobiological foundation of nurturing, caregiving, and parental love. Its roots lie in the hypothalamus, anterior cingulate cortex, and ventral tegmental area, regions enriched with oxytocin, prolactin, and endogenous opioids. This system fosters bonding and protects offspring, engaging deep subcortical pathways that support maternal behavior and emotional warmth.

Panic/Grief

PANIC/GRIEF is the emotional signature of separation and social loss. It is encoded in the anterior cingulate cortex, periaqueductal gray, and dorsal thalamus. Neurochemically, it is modulated by endogenous opioids, oxytocin, and CRF, substances that signal distress and regulate social pain. These circuits underscore the emotional cost of isolation and the deep biological need for connection.

Play

The PLAY system brings joy, social bonding, and learning through movement and interaction. Anchored in the dorsal thalamus, periaqueductal gray, and cerebellum, it is energized by dopamine and endogenous opioids. PLAY helps young mammals develop social fluency and resilience, and it remains vital in adult life as a source of joy and adaptability. Its anatomical roots lie in motor and affective subcortical networks.

A. D. (Bud) Craig and the Interoceptive Self

Perhaps the best way to experience Bud Craig is by reading his last book that summarized over 30 years of his research program. *How Do You Feel? An Interoceptive Moment with Your Neurobiological Self* (Craig, 2009) was his reinterpretation of the foundations of human emotion, consciousness, and the sense of self. He argued that all emotions are rooted in the brain's representation of the body's internal physiological state. Departing from traditional views that locate the essence of consciousness in exteroceptive awareness (seeing, hearing, and touching), Craig insisted that what truly defines our sentient existence is interoception: The moment-to-moment perception of what is happening inside the body.

At the heart of Craig's theory is a specific neural pathway that transmits interoceptive signals from the body to the brain. This system, known as the lamina I spinothalamocortical pathway, relays sensory information from the spinal cord to the posterior insula of the cerebral cortex. There, the brain constructs a dynamic map of the internal bodily state or a kind of neural "image" of the self, constantly updated with input about temperature, pain, hunger, heart rate, and other homeostatic signals.

Craig emphasized that this representation does not remain isolated in the posterior insula. Rather, it is relayed forward to the anterior insula, where these bodily sensations are integrated, interpreted, and ultimately transformed into conscious feeling states. It is here, in the anterior insula, that Craig located the seat of sentient self-awareness and the place where the body becomes felt as "mine" and where emotions are consciously experienced. In this framework, the anterior insula emerges not as a mere relay station but as a central hub for constructing emotional awareness, time perception, empathy, and the embodied sense of self.

Emotion, in Craig's view, is neither purely cognitive nor purely reactive, it is the experience of homeostatic imbalance, tracked and signaled by interoceptive systems. Feelings arise when the brain detects a deviation from physiological balance, processes that deviation through insular networks, and generates the subjective sense that "something is wrong" or "something is needed". In this way, emotion is grounded not in abstract appraisal but in the biological imperative of maintaining life.

This perspective has deep evolutionary roots. Craig traced how the neural systems responsible for interoception and emotional awareness developed across species, with the increasing complexity of insular circuitry marking a turning point in the emergence of consciousness. The human capacity for self-awareness, he argued, is inseparable from this capacity to feel the body and to register, interpret, and give meaning to its internal signals.

Craig's work became a proposal for a new model of the self. It placed the body at the center of emotional life and challenged the division between mind and body. Consciousness, Craig contended, is not a detached observer of bodily states; it *is* the felt narrative of those states. In a single interoceptive moment, we do not simply know, we feel ourselves into existence (Craig, 2010).

Antonio Damasio and the Somatic Marker Hypothesis

Jaak Panksepp and Bud Craig's research parallels nicely with another great scientist in affective neuroscience, Antonio Damasio. He has demonstrated that emotions are not separate from rational thought but integral to it (Damasio, 1994; 1999). His research bridges neuroscience, psychology, and philosophy, and centers on the idea that emotions are biological processes rooted in the body and brain and are essential for decision-making, social behavior, and consciousness.

One of Damasio's most influential contributions comes from his study of patients with damage to the ventromedial prefrontal cortex, a brain area critical for emotion processing. These individuals often retained high intelligence and reasoning ability but exhibited poor decision-making in real-life situations. This paradox led Damasio to develop his "somatic marker hypothesis". According to this theory, emotions function as somatic (bodily) signals that guide behavior and decision-making. These markers are the brain's way of assigning value to possible choices, based on past emotional experiences. Without these signals, decision-making becomes irrational, despite intact logic.

In his book *Descartes' Error* (1994) Damasio famously argues against the dualistic separation of mind and body, showing instead that the body converses to the brain through a continuous flow of interoceptive and emotional feedback. Emotions, in this view, are not irrational intrusions, they evolved as adaptive responses that allow organisms to survive, navigate complex environments, and form social bonds.

Damasio goes a little further by distinguishing between emotions and feelings: Emotions are unconscious bodily responses (like changes in heart rate or hormonal shifts), while feelings are the conscious experience of those responses. This distinction allows him to frame consciousness as arising from the brain's representation of the body's emotional states. Essentially, we "feel" ourselves into awareness.

In his later work, especially in *The Feeling of What Happens* (1999) and *Self Comes to Mind*, (2010) Damasio explores how consciousness develops from the integration of emotional and interoceptive signals in the brainstem and insular cortex. He proposes that the core-self arises from moment-to-moment representations of the body in relation to its environment, while the autobiographical self builds on memory and identity. Both are grounded in emotion.

Hugo Critchley and Heart Rate Variability

Hugo Critchley's research (2001; 2005; 2017) occupies a pivotal space at the intersection of neuroscience, emotion, and interoception, with a particular emphasis on how bodily states influence emotional and cognitive experience. Building on the theoretical groundwork laid by figures such as Antonio Damasio and Bud Craig, Critchley has helped empirically anchor the idea that the subjective feeling of emotion is inseparable from the physiological states of the body.

A central focus of Critchley's work is the role of the autonomic nervous system in emotional awareness. Using neuroimaging techniques, particularly functional MRI, he has demonstrated how changes in heart rate, blood pressure, and gut activity are not only tracked by the brain, but also integrated into emotional experience. His studies consistently highlight the anterior insula as a critical structure for interoceptive awareness. One of Critchley's key contributions is the demonstration that individuals vary in their ability to perceive internal signals; a capacity known as interoceptive sensitivity. This variability is not trivial because higher interoceptive sensitivity has been linked to heightened emotional awareness, greater anxiety, and increased empathic ability (Critchley & Garfinkel, 2017). Conversely, reduced interoceptive sensitivity is often observed in individuals with alexithymia or certain mood disorders. These findings underscore the relevance of interoception to diagnosis and treatment.

Critchley has also explored how interoception interacts with cognitive processes such as decision-making and attention. For example, his research shows that cardiac signals can influence risk-taking behavior and reaction time, suggesting that the "body loop" is not a passive background process but an active modulator of mental life. His findings point to a dynamic and reciprocal relationship between body and brain and one in which bodily rhythms continuously shape perception, emotion, and self-awareness (Critchley et al., 2001).

Through an elegant combination of physiological monitoring and neuroimaging, Critchley has provided compelling evidence that interoception forms a core scaffold for emotional experience. His work has broadened the scope of affective neuroscience, providing a rigorous empirical foundation for embodied models of the mind. In doing so, Critchley has reinforced a view of emotion that is not abstract or disembodied, but deeply physiological, moment-to-moment, and grounded in the living body.

Manos Tsakiris and Body Ownership

Manos Tsakiris's research (Tsakiris, 2017; Tsakiris & Depreester, 2018) represents a compelling fusion of neuroscience, cultural neuroscience, psychology, and philosophy, centered on the relationship between interoception, emotion, and the construction of the self. His work is foundational in shaping contemporary understandings of the "embodied self", a concept that situates identity and emotional awareness within the felt physiology of the body.

At the core of Tsakiris's research is the idea that emotions emerge from the integration of internal bodily signals with cognitive and perceptual processes. Much of his work focuses on how interoception, the sense of the body from within, contributes to our experience of selfhood. He argues that bodily awareness is not merely sensory data but a formative influence on who we are, how we feel, and how we relate to others.

Tsakiris has extensively investigated the neural mechanisms behind interoceptive awareness and their implications for emotional experience. Through neuroimaging studies and psychophysiological experiments, he has shown that the insular cortex plays a central role in transforming raw interoceptive signals into self-related feelings. In particular, his research reveals how disruptions in interoception can affect emotional regulation and contribute to psychiatric symptoms, such as depersonalization, anxiety, and depression.

His work is especially influential in exploring the malleability of body ownership and self-representation. Using paradigms like the rubber hand illusion, Tsakiris has demonstrated that the brain can rapidly revise its sense of bodily identity based on the integration, or disintegration, of interoceptive and exteroceptive signals. These findings have profound implications for understanding how emotional experiences and bodily awareness contribute to the integrity of the self.

Importantly, Tsakiris also extends his work into social and cultural contexts. He explores how social exclusion, discrimination, or political ideologies may alter bodily awareness and emotional processing, suggesting that interoceptive and emotional experience is not only biological but also deeply shaped by lived experience. This research bridges the gap between affective neuroscience and social cognition, highlighting the embeddedness of the self in a social and bodily context.

In sum, Tsakiris's work invites us to reconsider emotion not as an abstract psychological state, but as an embodied phenomenon that arises from, and helps define, the self. His research gives voice to the silent physiological currents that underlie our sense of being and underscores the importance of body-based processes in emotion, identity, and mental health.

Ralph Adolphs and David J. Anderson and Evolutionary Neuroscience

In *The Neuroscience of Emotion: A New Synthesis* (2018) Ralph Adolphs and David J. Anderson offer a bold and integrative framework for understanding emotion from a systems neuroscience perspective. Challenging long-standing psychological models and categorical theories of emotion, the authors propose a biologically grounded, functionally driven approach that emphasizes emotion as a set of internal states evolved to solve adaptive problems and not fixed responses or abstract mental categories.

Adolphs and Anderson begin by dismantling traditional emotion theories that rely heavily on discrete categories like fear, anger, or happiness. They argue that such classifications, though intuitive and historically entrenched, lack a consistent neural or evolutionary basis. Instead, they advocate for a framework rooted in circuits, computation, and evolution, which is a biologically plausible model of emotion that avoids circular reasoning.

Central to their thesis is the idea that emotions are constructed by the brain from more fundamental components that are core affective processes, physiological drives, and contextual information. These components are orchestrated by interacting neural circuits, particularly those in the hypothalamus, amygdala, and brainstem. The authors argue that rather than asking "Where is fear in the brain?" we should ask, "What are the circuits that regulate defensive behaviors, and how do they interact with perception, memory, and context?"

The book draws on research across species to trace the conserved and divergent features of emotional circuitry. By emphasizing cross-species comparisons, Adolphs and Anderson offer a truly evolutionary neuroscience of emotion; one that links neural circuits to survival-relevant behaviors and avoids human-centric assumptions.

Importantly, they distinguish between emotion states and emotion concepts. Emotion states are brain–body responses that guide behavior, while emotion concepts are the culturally shaped, language-mediated categories we use to describe them. This distinction allows the authors to reconcile the variability of emotional experience with the underlying stability of brain mechanisms.

Adolphs and Anderson advocate for a multi-level, interdisciplinary science of emotion that integrates systems neuroscience, ethology, psychology, and computational modeling. They call for precision in language, rigor in experiment design, and caution in interpreting correlations between brain activity and subjective reports. By reorienting the field around circuits and behavior, Adolphs and Anderson offer a vision of affective neuroscience that is biologically principled, methodologically rigorous, and intellectually expansive. Their work invites us to move beyond categories and toward a deeper understanding of emotion as an embodied, context-sensitive, and evolutionarily grounded phenomenon.

Elizabeth Johnston and Lea Olson: Biology and Experience

In *The Feeling Brain: The Biology and Psychology of Emotions* (2015), Elizabeth Johnston and Leah Olson provide a comprehensive and accessible exploration of how brain biology gives rise to emotional experience. Merging neurobiological mechanisms with psychological theory, they demystify emotion by grounding it in the workings of neural systems, neurotransmitters, and bodily processes without losing sight of the subjective and social dimensions of emotional life.

Johnston and Olson unpack the evolutionary roots of emotion and emphasize that emotions evolved as adaptive responses to challenges related to survival, reproduction, and social living. These are not luxuries of cognition, but core functions of the brain. Drawing on comparative studies, they show that emotional processing systems are conserved across species and closely tied to subcortical structures such as the amygdala, hypothalamus, and periaqueductal gray.

A major theme of the book is the interplay between biology and experience. Johnston and Olson explore how emotions emerge from the dynamic interaction between brain systems and lived environments. In addition, their treatment of specific emotions is framed not in isolation but within broader regulatory systems, including the autonomic nervous system and hormonal feedback loops and how these systems help the organism respond flexibly to environmental demands.

Johnston and Olson give careful attention to the cultural aspects of emotion in how language, identity, gender, and social norms mediate emotional experience. They adopt powerful biopsychosocial perspective that honors both the neurobiology of emotion and its richly contextual human expression.

Stephen Porges and Polyvagal Theory

Stephen Porges's groundbreaking work on the Polyvagal Theory (Porges, 2011; 2017) has redefined our understanding of the autonomic nervous system and its role in emotional regulation, social behavior, and trauma. At the heart of his theory is a profound reconceptualization of the vagus nerve not as a unitary structure, but as a system composed of evolutionarily distinct branches that support different modes of physiological and emotional response.

Porges argues that the autonomic nervous system is hierarchically organized, reflecting the evolutionary history of vertebrates. The most ancient system, the dorsal vagal complex, is associated with immobilization responses such as freezing or shutdown in the face of extreme threat. The sympathetic nervous system supports mobilization, including fight-or-flight behaviors. Most novel and uniquely mammalian is the ventral vagal complex, which underlies social engagement, facial expression, vocalization, and heart rate regulation through the myelinated vagus.

What distinguishes the Polyvagal Theory is its emphasis on the "neuroception" of safety, a pre-conscious evaluation of risk that governs shifts between autonomic states. According to Porges, our physiological state determines the range of emotions and behaviors available to us: We can only access calm social engagement when the nervous system detects safety and activates the ventral vagal system. Conversely, perceived threat can trigger defensive states, even in the absence of conscious awareness.

Porges's work has had profound implications for the understanding and treatment of trauma, developmental disorders, and affective dysregulation. His theory provides a neurobiological explanation for why individuals with histories of chronic stress or trauma may become "stuck" in defensive physiological states, limiting their capacity for connection, regulation, and emotional expression.

Importantly, Porges brings an embodied framework to the study of emotion and behavior, highlighting how core emotional processes are deeply rooted in the body's physiological organization. He draws attention to the bidirectional communication between body and brain, especially the role of cardiac vagal tone as a marker of emotional flexibility and resilience.

His contributions extend beyond theory into practice, influencing therapeutic approaches that emphasize co-regulation, breathwork, prosodic voice, and safe relational contexts as tools for restoring autonomic balance. The Polyvagal Theory invites a shift away from pathologizing behavior toward understanding the biological imperatives behind emotional states. Stephen Porges's research affirms that emotional life is not simply cognitive or cultural, it is visceral, rhythmic, and deeply embedded in the neurophysiological architecture of the human body.

The Human Affectome Project

The Human Affectome Project is a collaborative effort to map the emotional landscape of the human brain (Schiller et al., 2022). It brings together researchers from more than 23 countries under the coordination of the International Neuroinformatics Coordinating Facility in Canada. The Affectome researchers come from a variety of backgrounds: neuroscience, psychology, computational biology, psychiatry, and philosophy. Their shared mission is to create a comprehensive picture of human affect by combining neuroscience, data science, and decades of research on emotion.

The term "affect" in this context covers the full range of emotional experience such as basic emotions, moods, personality traits, and bodily states. The Human Affectome Project embraces the complexity of the emotional brain, acknowledging that emotions come from layered, interacting systems that include ancient brainstem circuits and modern cortical structures.

The project is unfolding in two big phases. First, researchers have conducted a massive literature review (analyzing over 3,000 scientific articles) to identify and organize more than 100 different affective terms. These terms are grouped into categories such as core emotions, moods, affective traits, and body-related feelings. For each one, the team mapped out where it shows up in the brain, which neurotransmitters are involved, and what kind of bodily reactions are tied to it. This has created a working taxonomy, a sort of roadmap for how we experience affect.

In the second phase, the team is using neuroimaging data and computational models to link this taxonomy to actual brain networks. They have found that while emotion-related activity is spread out across the brain, certain areas keep coming up again and again especially the anterior insula, anterior cingulate cortex, amygdala, hypothalamus, and periaqueductal gray. These structures turn out to be key hubs where affective processing overlaps with self-awareness, decision-making, and social behavior. The project also shows that these regions interact with larger brain networks like the default mode network and salience network, which further blurs the line between feeling and thinking.

One of the project's biggest contributions is its introduction of the word "affectome" that is a way to describe the full system of emotional functions and brain regions involved in affect. The affectome is not static. It changes as we grow, depending on our biology, our experiences, and our social lives. This idea pushes emotion research away from simple categories like "happy" or "sad" and toward a more flexible, real-world understanding of how emotions actually work.

At its core, the Human Affectome Project shows that emotion is a constantly shifting process that links body, brain, and environment in a dynamic system. The work has big implications not just for neuroscience, but for therapy, mental health, AI, and how we think about being human in a connected world.

Connections to Cultural Neuroscience

The establishment of the Human Affectome Project is influencing multiple fields of neuroscientific inquiry and is helping to establish an expectation that cultural variables should be included pervasively across research and practice. It intersects with another avenue for inquiry that has been coined "Cultural Neuroscience".

Cultural Neuroscience is an emerging interdisciplinary field that explores how culture and biology dynamically shape the human brain, mind, and behavior across the lifespan. Drawing from cognitive neuroscience, psychology, anthropology, and genetics, it examines how cultural values, practices, and environments influence neural processes such as perception, emotion, and social cognition and how these brain mechanisms, in turn, reinforce and perpetuate cultural norms. This bidirectional framework highlights that neither culture nor biology operates in isolation; instead, they interact continuously to mold neural architecture and behavioral tendencies. Cultural neuroscience helps explain individual and group differences in cognition, emotion regulation, and mental health outcomes. The following sections provide short summaries of cultural neuroscientific perspectives on sex/gender, socioeconomic, and racial/ethnic differences in emotional functioning. This information is representative of progress but is certainly not definitive. We can look forward to future collaboration with other areas of neuroscience and this will help consolidate a biopsychosocial model across the many arms of the field.

Sex and Gender Differences in Emotional Functioning

Sex and gender differences are shaped by developmental stage, cultural context, and individual experience (Ellison & Nelson, 2009). Recent studies confirm modest but reliable sex-related differences in certain brain regions involved in emotional processing. For example, females tend to show increased gray matter density in areas such as the anterior cingulate cortex, insula, and orbitofrontal cortex that are regions implicated in emotion regulation and interoception. Males show relatively higher amygdala volume and more hierarchical network organization across brain systems (Hamann, 2005; Stevens & Hamann, 2012). These differences may support sex-specific patterns in how emotion is processed and regulated, though the magnitude of these anatomical differences is generally small and should not be overinterpreted.

Emerging research indicates nuanced sex-related variation in neurotransmitter function. Females appear to have lower baseline serotonin synthesis but increased responsiveness to serotonergic interventions. Dopaminergic activity, especially in reward pathways, is often higher in males, whereas females show stronger responses to social and emotional rewards. New studies have identified that immune cells in females may release endogenous opioids in response to estrogen and progesterone following injury, providing a potential sex-specific mechanism for pain modulation (Cosgrove et al., 2007).

Oxytocin and vasopressin systems show consistent sex-based differences. Females typically show higher oxytocin receptor density in regions linked to bonding and empathy. In contrast, vasopressin is more prominent in males, with links to social vigilance and defensive aggression. Estrogen has a well-documented role in modulating serotonin and oxytocin activity, while testosterone is associated with amygdala activation and assertiveness. However, hormonal effects vary significantly across developmental stages and within individuals (Dumais & Veenema, 2016).

Functional imaging studies reveal that girls and women tend to show increased amygdala and anterior cingulate cortex activation to emotionally ambiguous or stressful stimuli, whereas boys and men may exhibit dampened responses under chronic stress. These findings suggest potential sex differences in how emotional salience and stress are processed, but findings should be viewed in context of developmental timing, cultural influences, and individual experience (Bangasser & Wicks, 2017).

While sex differences in emotion-related neurobiology exist, they are generally modest and modulated by developmental, hormonal, and environmental influences. These findings highlight the importance of considering sex and gender as one part of a complex biopsychosocial model in emotional development and mental health. Clinicians should be cautious not to pathologize individual differences through a binary lens and should remain aware of how sex interacts with sociocultural context and lived experience.

Sex and gender differences influence how individuals respond to psychotropic medications, including antidepressants, stimulants, and anxiolytics (Soldin & Mattinson, 2009). Females often show heightened sensitivity to serotonergic medications and may require lower doses due to differences in drug metabolism, hormone interactions, and body composition. For example, estrogen can enhance the efficacy of SSRIs, whereas progesterone may attenuate it. Males, by contrast, may exhibit stronger dopaminergic responses, influencing the effectiveness and side effects of stimulant and antipsychotic medications (Becker & Chartoff, 2019). Additionally, sex-specific genetic polymorphisms in cytochrome P450 enzymes (such as CYP3A4 and CYP2D6) can alter drug metabolism, leading to variations in plasma concentrations (Soldin & Mattison, 2009). These differences underscore the importance of sex-informed prescribing practices and ongoing monitoring to optimize both efficacy and tolerability. Sex and gender differences are shaped by developmental stage, cultural context, and individual experience.

Socioeconomic Status and Emotional Functioning

Socioeconomic status (SES) influences brain development, neurochemistry, and emotional functioning (Blair & Raver, 2016). SES is a powerful social determinant of health, and its impact on the developing brain is multifaceted affecting structure, connectivity, stress regulation, and emotional outcomes. While SES is not destiny, it shapes the environment in which neurodevelopment occurs and can amplify or buffer risk factors for emotional dysregulation.

Children from lower SES backgrounds tend to show differences in brain structure and function, particularly in regions involved in emotional regulation, language, and executive function. Studies consistently report smaller volumes in the prefrontal cortex, hippocampus, and anterior cingulate cortex, areas essential for self-regulation and stress modulation (Nobel et al., 2015). These structural differences are thought to result from a combination of factors including chronic stress exposure, reduced access to enriching experiences, and environmental instability.

Lower SES is associated with chronic activation of the hypothalamic-pituitary-adrenal (HPA) axis, leading to elevated cortisol levels and altered autonomic nervous system function. This dysregulation can sensitize limbic regions such as the amygdala and impair the buffering capacity of the prefrontal cortex. Over time, children living in high-stress, low-resource environments may become more emotionally reactive and less able to return to baseline after distress (Blair & Raver, 2016).

Socioeconomic adversity has been linked to alterations in neurotransmitter systems. Early exposure to chronic stress can reduce dopamine availability in reward pathways, contributing to anhedonia or motivational impairments (Evans & Kim, 2013). Low serotonin function has also been observed in children under chronic stress, increasing vulnerability to mood and anxiety disorders (Pizzagalli, 2014). Nutritional deficits common in low-resource environments may also influence GABA and glutamate balance, further affecting emotional reactivity and regulation (Georgieff, 2007).

Children from lower SES contexts are more likely to exhibit emotional dysregulation, heightened vigilance, impulsivity, or flattened affect. These patterns are not simply behavioral; they reflect adaptive responses to unpredictability and threat. Emotional coping may become narrowed, favoring fight, flight, or freeze responses over reflection or problem-solving. Such adaptations are functional in high-stress environments but may be misinterpreted or pathologized in educational and clinical settings (Fletcher-Janzen & Harrington, 2021).

Not all children from low SES backgrounds show negative outcomes. Protective factors such as responsive caregiving, stable routines, community support, and access to early enrichment programs can buffer against neurodevelopmental risk. These supports help strengthen prefrontal-limbic connectivity, enhance emotional resilience, and promote neuroplasticity. The presence of even one emotionally attuned adult can dramatically alter developmental trajectories (Blair & Raver, 2016).

SES can indirectly affect psychopharmacological outcomes through disparities in access, adherence, and health literacy. Children from lower SES backgrounds may face barriers to consistent medication management, such as unstable housing, inconsistent follow-up, or lack of insurance coverage (Evans & Kim, 2013). In addition, chronic stress and poor nutrition, which are more common in low-resource environments, can alter liver enzyme activity and gut microbiota, potentially impacting medication absorption and metabolism (Borre et al., 2014).

Clinicians must consider these contextual variables when prescribing, educating families, and monitoring treatment effects. Psychopharmacologic interventions should be embedded in a broader framework of care that includes attention to environmental stressors, caregiver support, and equitable access to healthcare services.

Socioeconomic status is a critical factor in emotional development, shaping brain structure, stress systems, and coping patterns. Clinicians must consider the neurobiological impact of poverty, instability, and chronic stress when working with children from low-SES backgrounds. Interventions should prioritize emotional safety, sensory regulation, and relational attunement before emphasizing cognitive or behavioral goals. Understanding the neuroscience of SES allows us to reframe "problem behavior" as adaptive neurodevelopmental responses to adversity.

Racial and Ethnic Factors in Emotional Functioning

This summary reviews current research on how race and ethnicity influence brain development, emotional regulation, and neuropsychological functioning. While race and ethnicity tend to be used as social constructs without direct biological grounding, they intersect powerfully with lived experiences of discrimination, cultural identity, and access to resources. These factors shape developmental trajectories through psychosocial stress, environmental exposures, and sociocultural context.

Emerging studies suggest that racial and ethnic minority children may exhibit differences in brain development, particularly in regions associated with stress response, emotion regulation, and executive functioning (Kral et al., 2024; Assari et al., 2020). These patterns are likely driven by environmental exposures such as chronic discrimination, socioeconomic disadvantage, neighborhood stress, and educational inequity rather than innate biology. Reduced volume or altered connectivity in the amygdala, prefrontal cortex, and hippocampus has been observed in marginalized populations, often associated with cumulative stress and trauma exposure.

Experiences of racism, implicit bias, and microaggressions contribute to chronic activation of the HPA axis and sustained elevations in cortisol. These physiological stress responses may sensitize limbic circuits and alter emotional reactivity (Berger et al., 2018). Children and adolescents from marginalized communities frequently navigate racialized environments that demand vigilance and emotional suppression that can impair emotional flexibility and increase internalizing or externalizing symptoms (Hicken et al., 2013; Priest et al., 2013).

Racial and ethnic differences in psychopharmacological response are increasingly recognized in both pediatric and adult populations. These differences may arise from genetic polymorphisms affecting drug metabolism, as well as from social determinants that impact medication access, adherence, and therapeutic relationships. For example, variations in certain enzymes (e.g. CYP2D6, CYP2C19) can influence metabolism of antidepressants, stimulants, and antipsychotics, leading to differences in drug efficacy and side-effect profiles across populations (Brody et.al., 2014; Strickland et al., 2000).

Emotion expression and regulation are shaped by cultural norms, values, and parenting practices. Some cultures emphasize emotional restraint and harmony, while others encourage expressiveness or communal processing of emotion. These cultural frameworks shape how children learn to interpret, communicate, and manage emotional experiences. Clinicians must recognize that behaviors considered "dysregulated" in one context may reflect cultural norms in another.

Structural racism contributes to disparities in education, healthcare access, environmental safety, and early childhood enrichment, all of which, influence brain development and emotional health. Children from marginalized communities are disproportionately exposed to adverse childhood experiences, school discipline, and biased assessments. These systemic factors shape not only outcomes but also the interpretation of behaviors by teachers, clinicians, and institutions (Fletcher-Janzen & Harrington, 2021).

Despite these challenges, racial and ethnic communities possess strong cultural protective factors. These include extended family networks, faith-based support, cultural pride, communal storytelling, and resilience practices passed down through generations. Affirming cultural identity has been shown to buffer the effects of discrimination and enhance emotional regulation, self-esteem, and neurodevelopmental resilience (Umana-Taylor et al., 2021).

Racial and ethnic identity interacts with emotional development through cultural, environmental, and structural pathways. Clinicians must consider the impact of discrimination, cultural norms, and systemic inequities when evaluating emotional and behavioral concerns. Culturally attuned practice, which is grounded in humility, inclusion, and respect, can promote more accurate assessment, build trust, and support children in developing emotionally rich and resilient lives.

General Limitations of Neuroscientific Research: Things to Keep in Mind

Researchers are also confined by the parameters of how we investigate the brain. This means that we should all be wary of accepting ideas about how brain functioning plays out in everyday life. Research to practice is a very long distance, and in that light, we should mention some of the limitations of neuroscientific and imaging studies about emotions. Neuroscience, like all disciplines, is constrained by its methods and while those methods have grown very sophisticated, they are far from perfect. This is especially true in the study of emotion. Imaging tools such as fMRI, PET, and EEG have offered profound insights into the neural underpinnings of affect, but they provide only fragments of a much larger story. Moving from research findings to meaningful clinical application requires both critical thinking and an appreciation for what these technologies cannot tell us as well as what we hope to infer (Barrett & Satpute, 2013; Poldrack, 2008).

Correlation vs. Causation

A fundamental limitation of imaging research is that most studies are correlational. When we see activity in the amygdala in response to a fearful face, it does not mean the amygdala alone is generating fear. The human brain does not function as a set of discrete "emotion buttons" labeled sad, happy, or angry. Emotions are emergent phenomena, arising from dynamic interactions across distributed neural networks and interactions that extend beyond the brain into the body and environment (Pessoa, 2008). Teaching students to resist the allure of oversimplification with correlational data interpretation is crucial for developing sophisticated clinical reasoning.

Temporal Constraints

Another critical limitation is temporal resolution. Emotional processes occur in milliseconds and are fast, embodied, and often beneath conscious awareness. Yet fMRI, our workhorse for functional imaging, captures data over seconds, which is painfully slow in neural terms. We see the echo of an emotion, not the flashpoint that initiates it (Logothetis, 2008). For students and researchers, this underscores the need to interpret imaging data with humility because we are not observing the "raw" emotion, but rather a delayed and often averaged signal.

Artificiality of Lab Tasks

Many imaging paradigms reduce complex affective experiences to simplified stimuli such as looking at photographs of facial expressions or listening to a brief audio clip. While these tasks are useful for controlling experimental variables, they are also stripped of context and depth. Real-world emotions, particularly in children, arise from relational, sensory, and environmental factors that simply cannot be replicated in the sterile environment of a scanner (Krakauer et al., 2017; Immordino-Yang & Damasio, 2007). Translating lab-based findings to clinical realities requires bridging this gap.

Reverse Inference

Reverse inference is another methodological pitfall. The fact that a particular brain region is active does not reveal the subjective experience of the individual. For example, the insula is involved in disgust, empathy, bodily awareness, and pain perception. Its activation does not tell us which of these processes is occurring at a given moment. Without behavioral data or subjective report, we risk attributing far more certainty to these findings than the data can support (Poldrack, 2006; Hutzler, 2014).

Sample Bias and Developmental Gaps

A persistent problem in neuroscience is that the majority of imaging research is conducted most often young adult university students. This means that findings are rarely representative of children, adolescents, older adults, or individuals from diverse cultural and socioeconomic backgrounds (Henrich et al., 2010). Developmental trajectories, trauma histories, neurodivergent conditions, and cultural factors all influence how emotions are expressed and regulated. Yet these critical variables are frequently missing from the datasets that shape our theoretical models (Falk et al., 2013).

Cost, Accessibility, and Practical Relevance

Finally, these imaging technologies are costly, time-intensive, and largely inaccessible to most clinical and educational settings. Even when the data are available, the leap from imaging findings to practical interventions is rarely straightforward. A scan might tell us that a child's amygdala is hyper-responsive to threat cues, but it will not tell us how to build the sense of safety, trust, and regulation that child needs (Satel & Lilienfeld, 2013; Poldrack, 2008).

The Body Is Missing from the Picture

A major conceptual limitation is the lingering dualism in neuroscientific research. Too often, studies treat the brain as if it operates in isolation, overlooking the fact that emotions are embodied phenomena. Interoception plays a fundamental role in affective experience. A. Bud Craig's pioneering work has helped integrate the body into our models of emotion, but many studies still fail to consider how heart rate, gut signals, hormonal fluctuations, and sensory systems contribute to emotional regulation.

In summary, neuroscience's reliance on neuroimaging provides pieces of a puzzle that must be integrated with behavioral observations, developmental knowledge, cultural context, and lived experience. Imaging can inform us about activation patterns or neuroanatomical correlates, but it cannot replace the clinician's ability to listen, observe, and build trust. While neuroimaging can deepen our respect for the biological basis of emotion, it should not be mistaken for the whole map. As clinicians, we are still called to listen to bodies, stories, and lived experience. We are clinicians who have an N=1 in front of us and while a single-case-subject design is at the root of our practice, we still practice heart-to-heart (literally!). The most effective use of neuroimaging research data, therefore, is in integrative models that are biopsychosocial in nature.

When conducting the Affective Inventory that is described in later chapters, it is important to know each of the core emotional systems in depth before trying to translate them into counseling goals. The purpose of this book is to help the clinician identify and explore core emotions in a structured and safe manner. Helping a client figure out what core emotion is driving an issue leads directly to understanding the function of the feelings. For example, if the client expresses anger, they are defending something. What are they defending? Why do they feel the need to defend? Is defending the best strategy? Core emotions, once identified, are a compass that direct us down to the functional point of origin and then back up to real-life applications. The following seven chapters go through each of Panksepp's core emotions summarizing neuroanatomical, neurochemical, and allostatic features. Each section also explores the breadth of the emotion, the translation of the emotion into real-life, Therapeutic Touchpoints for counseling goals for the clinician, and lastly a take-away handout for the client. The touchpoints and client handouts are included in the body of the chapter so that the reader can see how the activities might translate into a session. Copies of the handouts that are reproducible for the client can be found on the book's webpage at: www.routledge.com/9781041250135

References

Adolphs, R., & Anderson, D. J. (2018). *The neuroscience of emotion: A new synthesis*. Princeton University Press.

Assari, S., Boyce, S., Bazargan, M., & Caldwell, C. H. (2020). African American children's diminished returns of parental educational attainment on their cognitive ability. *Frontiers in Education*, 5, 110.

Bangasser, D. A., & Wicks, B. (2017). Sex-specific mechanisms for responding to stress. *Journal of Neuroscience Research*, 95(1–2), 75–82.

Barrett, L. F., & Satpute, A. B. (2013). Large-scale brain networks in affective and social neuroscience: Towards an integrative functional architecture of the brain. *Current Opinion in Neurobiology*, 23(3), 361–372.

Becker, J. B., & Chartoff, E. (2019). Sex differences in neural mechanisms mediating reward and addiction. *Neuropsychopharmacology*, 44(1), 166–183.

Berger, M., Sarnyai, Z., & Lundberg, U. (2018). Stress, depression and the HPA axis: A role for racial discrimination? *Psychoneuroendocrinology*, 91, 98–106.

Blair, C., & Raver, C. C. (2016). Poverty, stress, and brain development: New directions for prevention and intervention. *Academic Pediatrics*, 16(3), S30–S36.

Borre, Y. E., O'Keeffe, G. W., Clarke, G., Stanton, C., Dinan, T. G., & Cryan, J. F. (2014). Microbiota and neurodevelopmental windows: Implications for brain disorders. *Trends in Molecular Medicine*, 20(9), 509–518.

Brody, A. L., Saxena, S., Mandelkern, M. A., Fairbanks, L. A., Ho, M. L., & Baxter, L. R. (2014). Brain metabolic changes during pharmacologic treatment of depression: A PET study. *Journal of Clinical Psychiatry*, 65(8), 1102–1108.

Cosgrove, K. P., Mazure, C. M., & Staley, J. K. (2007). Evolving knowledge of sex differences in brain structure, function, and chemistry. *Biological Psychiatry*, 62(8), 847–855.

Craig, A. D. (2009). *How do you feel? An interoceptive moment with your neurobiological self*. Princeton University Press.

Craig, A. D. (2010). The sentient self. *Brain Structure and Function*, 214(5–6), 563–577. https://doi.org/10.1007/s00429-010-0248-y

Critchely, H. (2005). Neural mechanisms of autonomic, affective, and cognitive integration. *Journal of Comparative Neurology*, 493, 54–166.

Critchley, H. D., & Garfinkel, S. N. (2017). Interoception and emotion. *Current Opinion in Psychology*, 17, 7–14. https://doi.org/10.1016/j.copsyc.2017.04.020

Critchley, H. D., Mathias, C. J., & Dolan, R. J. (2001). Neural activity in the human brain relating to uncertainty and arousal during anticipation. *Science*, 293(5527), 312–315.

Damasio, A. (1994). *Descartes' error: Emotion, reason, and the human brain*. Putnam & Sons.

Damasio, A. (1999). *The feeling of what happens: Body and emotion in the making of consciousness*. Harcourt Brace.

Dumais, K. M., & Veenema, A. H. (2016). Vasopressin and oxytocin receptor systems in the brain: Sex differences and sex-specific regulation of social behavior. *Frontiers in Neuroendocrinology*, 40, 1–23.

Ellison, P. T., & Nelson, R. J. (2009). *Reproductive ecology and human evolution*. Transition Publishers.

Evans, G. W., & Kim, P. (2013). Childhood poverty, chronic stress, self-regulation, and coping. *Child Development Perspectives*, 7(1), 43–48.

Falk, E. B., Hyde, L. W., Mitchell, C., Faul, J., Gonzalez, R., Heitzeg, M. M., & Schulenberg, J. (2013). What is a representative brain? Neuroscience meets population science. *Proceedings of the National Academy of Sciences*, 110(44), 17615–17622.

Fletcher-Janzen, E., & Harrington, E. (2021). Translating ACE research into multi-tiered systems of supports for at-risk high-school students. *Journal of Pediatric Neuropsychology*, 7, (89–101).

Georgieff, M. K. (2007). Nutrition and the developing brain: Nutrient priorities and measurement. *The American Journal of Clinical Nutrition*, 85(2), 614–620.

Hamann, S. (2005). Sex differences in the responses of the human amygdala. *Neuroscientist*, 11(4), 288–293.
Henrich, J., Heine, S. J., & Norenzayan, A. (2010). The weirdest people in the world? *Behavioral and Brain Sciences*, 33(2–3), 61–83.
Hicken, M. T., Lee, H., Ailshire, J., Burgard, S. A., & Williams, D. R. (2013). "Every shut eye, ain't sleep": The role of racism-related vigilance in racial/ethnic disparities in sleep difficulty. *Race and Social Problems*, 5(2), 100–112.
Hutzler, F. (2014). Reverse inference is not a fallacy per se: Cognitive processes can be inferred from functional imaging data. *NeuroImage*, 84, 1061–1069.
Immordino-Yang, M. H., & Damasio, A. (2007). We feel, therefore we learn: The relevance of affective and social neuroscience to education. *Mind, Brain, and Education*, 1(1), 3–10.
Johnston, E., & Olson, L. (2015). *The feeling brain: The biology and psychology of emotions*. W. W. Norton.
Krakauer, J. W., Ghazanfar, A. A., Gomez-Marin, A., MacIver, M. A., & Poeppel, D. (2017). Neuroscience needs behavior: Correcting a reductionist bias. *Neuron*, 93(3), 480–490.
Kral , T.R.A., Kesebir, P., Redford, L., Dahl, C.J., Wilson-Mendenhall, C.D., Hirshberg, M.J., et al. (2024). Healthy Minds Index: A brief measure of the core dimensions of well-being. *PLoS ONE* 19(5): e0299352.
Logothetis, N. K. (2008). What we can do and what we cannot do with fMRI. *Nature*, 453(7197), 869–878.
Noble, K.G., Houston, S.M., Brito N.H, Bartsch, H., Kan, E., Kuperman, J.M., Akshoomoff, N., Amaral, D.G., Bloss, C.S., Libiger, O., Schork ,N.J., Murray, S.S., Casey, B.J., Chang, L., Ernst, T.M., Frazier, J.A., Gruen, J.R., Kennedy, D.N., Van Zijl ,P., Mostofsky, S., Kaufmann ,W.E., Kenet ,T., Dale, A.M.., Jernigan, T.L., Sowell ,E.R. (2015). *Family income, parental education and brain structure in children and adolescents*. Nature Neuroscience 18(5):773-8.
Panksepp, J. (1998). *Affective neuroscience: The foundations of human and animal emotions*. Oxford University Press.
Panksepp, J., & Biven, L. (2012). *The archaeology of mind: Neuroevolutionary origins of human emotions*. W. W. Norton.
Pessoa, L. (2008). On the relationship between emotion and cognition. *Nature Reviews Neuroscience*, 9(2), 148–158.
Pizzagalli, D. A. (2014). Depression, stress, and anhedonia: Toward a synthesis and integrated model. *Annual Review of Clinical Psychology*, 10, 393–423.
Poldrack, R. A. (2006). Can cognitive processes be inferred from neuroimaging data? *Trends in Cognitive Sciences*, 10(2), 59–63.
Poldrack, R. A. (2008). The role of fMRI in cognitive neuroscience: Where do we stand? *Current Opinion in Neurobiology*, 18(2), 223–227.
Porges, S. W. (2011). *The polyvagal theory: Neurophysiological foundations of emotions, attachment, communication, and self-regulation*. W. W. Norton.
Porges, S. W. (2017). *The pocket guide to the polyvagal theory: The transformative power of feeling safe*. W. W. Norton.
Priest, N., Paradies, Y., Trenerry, B., Truong, M., Karlsen, S., & Kelly, Y. (2013). A systematic review of studies examining the relationship between reported racism and health and wellbeing for children and young people. *Social Science & Medicine*, 95, 115–127.
Satel, S., & Lilienfeld, S. O. (2013). *Brainwashed: The seductive appeal of mindless neuroscience*. Basic Books.
Schiller, D., Lowe, L., Becker, S., & Cromwell, H. (2022). *The human affectome project: Mapping emotion to brain and behavior*. Springer.
Soldin, O. P., & Mattison, D. R. (2009). Sex differences in pharmacokinetics and pharmacodynamics. *Clinical Pharmacokinetics*, 48(3), 143–157.
Stevens, J. S., & Hamann, S. (2012). Sex differences in brain activation to emotional stimuli: A meta-analysis of neuroimaging studies. *Neuropsychologia*, 50(7), 1578–1593.

Strickland, T. L., Burrell, M. J., & Richardson, L. A. (2000). Diversity in neuropsychology: A commentary on issues of assessment and training. *The Clinical Neuropsychologist*, 14(1), 21–32.

Tsakiris, M. (2017). The multisensory basis of the self: From body to identity to others. *The Quarterly Journal of Experimental Psychology*, *70*(4), 597–609.

Tsakiris, M., & De Preester, H. (Eds.) (2018). *The interoceptive mind: From homeostasis to awareness*. Oxford University Press.

Umana-Taylor, A. J., Kornienko, O., Douglass Bayless, S., & Updegraff, K. A. (2021). Ethnic identity and well-being in adolescence and young adulthood: A meta-analysis. *Developmental Psychology*, 57(4), 608–627.

Part II

Translating Panksepp's Seven Emotion Systems

Chapter 6

SEEKING

Development of SEEKING

Jaak Panksepp described the SEEKING system as a "goad without a goal" until it is partnered with other emotional systems (Panksepp, 2005a p. 32). A short history of how Panksepp demarked the SEEKING system is appropriate at this time because the idea of a distinct emotion of seeking is not a well-known construct. In addition, it is linked to not only all other emotions, but to areas of the brain (particularly the frontal lobes) that try to put meaning to our emotions.

Panksepp's discovery of the SEEKING system emerged from a careful and systematic study of motivated behaviors in animals, particularly rodents (1998a, 1998b, 2003, 2005a, 2005b, 2006a, 2006b; Panksepp & Biven, 2012). He was interested in understanding why animals often engaged in purposeful exploration even in the absence of immediate rewards such as food or safety. What appeared to be spontaneous and seemingly aimless activity revealed itself, upon closer inspection, to be driven by a deeper neural process. It was an intrinsic urge to investigate, to anticipate, and to engage with the world.

This line of inquiry led Panksepp and his colleagues to conduct experiments using deep brain stimulation. When they stimulated subcortical regions such as the ventral tegmental area (VTA), nucleus accumbens, and lateral hypothalamus, they observed a striking behavioral response. The animals became alert, energized, and goal oriented. They searched, sniffed, and explored as if driven by a powerful internal force. Perhaps most significantly, the animals would self-administer stimulation to these brain regions when given the opportunity, sometimes repeatedly for extended periods of time. This suggested that the activation of these circuits was inherently rewarding.

Although the neurotransmitter dopamine was already known to be involved in reward pathways, Panksepp proposed a crucial reinterpretation. Rather than viewing dopamine solely as the neurotransmitter of pleasure, he argued that it played a central role in the generation of anticipatory and appetitive behavior. The dopaminergic system, in his view, was not merely about the satisfaction of LUST, but about the emotional and motivational tone of expectation and engagement.

DOI: 10.4324/9781003745686-8

Panksepp named this emotional system SEEKING because it encapsulated the neuropsychological experience of curiosity, lust, foraging, investigation, and engagement with the environment. This system was not dependent on specific external goals; instead, it generated a generalized sense of enthusiasm, purpose, and readiness to encounter novel opportunities. It represented a foundational source of motivation, one that fuels learning, innovation, and exploration across the lifespan.

Over time, Panksepp and others (e.g. Davis & Montag, 2019) mapped the SEEKING system across mammalian species. They demonstrated that it involved a network of brain regions including the ventral tegmental area (VTA), nucleus accumbens, lateral hypothalamus, medial forebrain bundle (MFB), and prefrontal cortex. The system was shown to be centrally dopaminergic, but also modulated by other neurotransmitters and neuropeptides.

The implications of this discovery were significant. A dysregulated SEEKING system was found to be involved in conditions such as addiction, depression, and apathy, while a healthy and active SEEKING system supported emotional vitality, engagement with the world, and the pursuit of meaningful goals. For Panksepp, the SEEKING system was not only a neuroanatomical construct, but a core feature of emotional life. It represented the evolutionary foundation of our capacity to want, to wonder, and to act.

Allostatic Function of SEEKING

According to Panksepp the SEEKING system is a fundamental, energizing force that drives curiosity, motivation, and the urge to explore, even in the absence of a specific object or reward. It is central to his model of affective neuroscience and reflects the evolutionary importance of this system in adaptive behavior. This system does not just push us toward specific goals; it generates a state of active anticipation and psychological readiness. It is what animates the sense that "something good or essential might be out there, go find it".

The SEEKING system is a distinct affective system that weaves together a powerful mix of ideas and functions: wanting, needing, motivation, anticipation, exploration, craving, longing, curiosity, high arousal, problem-solving, strategy formation, appraisal, creativity, innovation, foraging, novelty-seeking, and the establishment of memories about resources for future use. It energizes goal-directed behavior and fuels inquisitiveness and the drive to make meaning. At its core, SEEKING is deeply connected to our sense of being alive and to our conscious sense of self. From an interoceptive perspective, SEEKING is foundational to decision-making and conscious feeling. Feelings of wanting and curiosity emerge as the brain's interpretation of internal body states that require resolution. It is an anticipatory system driving action toward restoring or enhancing internal balance.

Physiology and Neuroanatomical Features

Panksepp describes the SEEKING system as being rooted in ancient subcortical structures and follows the mesolimbic dopamine pathway. It originates in the VTA and projects to the nucleus accumbens, MFB, lateral hypothalamus, and prefrontal cortex. These regions work together to energize behavior, assess goals, and guide decision-making.

The key neurochemical that drives this system is dopamine, which fuels "wanting" and motivation but not necessarily pleasure itself. Other important neurochemicals include glutamate (facilitating cortical signaling), endogenous opioids (released upon reward attainment), orexin (which increases arousal and vigilance), and serotonin (which modulates impulsivity and helps regulate excessive drive).

Although the SEEKING system originates in subcortical regions, its full behavioral and psychological expression depends on how it interfaces with the frontal lobes. In particular, the medial and orbital regions of the prefrontal cortex play a critical role in shaping raw motivational energy into purposeful, context-sensitive action.

The medial prefrontal cortex receives dopaminergic input from the mesolimbic and mesocortical pathways and plays a central role in directing attention, organizing plans, and maintaining engagement with goals over time. When the SEEKING system is active, the medial prefrontal cortex helps coordinate that state of internal readiness into actions that are aligned with current needs and environmental opportunities. It translates appetitive arousal into structured, goal-directed behavior.

The orbitofrontal cortex contributes to this process by evaluating and assigning value to incoming sensory cues. This region allows the SEEKING system to adapt to changing conditions, guiding behavior toward the most meaningful, or rewarding possibilities in a given context. Rather than pursuing novelty indiscriminately, the brain begins to prioritize goals based on prior experience, outcome expectations, and learned associations.

In more complex forms of SEEKING, such as problem-solving or creative exploration, the dorsolateral prefrontal cortex supports working memory and sustained attention. It allows the individual to hold multiple steps in mind, inhibit distractions, and pursue abstract or long-range objectives. This region does not generate motivation itself but serves as a regulatory partner, organizing and maintaining the cognitive resources needed to act on the motivational signals initiated by the SEEKING system.

Finally, structures such as the ventromedial prefrontal cortex and anterior cingulate cortex help monitor internal conflict and adjust behavioral responses. These areas are involved in regulating the intensity of SEEKING, enabling shifts in strategy when initial efforts prove unsuccessful or when the anticipated outcome no longer aligns with internal goals.

In sum, Panksepp asserts that while the SEEKING system is rooted in subcortical mechanisms of dopaminergic arousal and exploration, it achieves its full adaptive potential only through its dynamic interplay with the frontal lobes. These cortical regions help the organism move from raw wanting to intentional action, from curiosity to insight, and from anticipation to fulfillment. This partnership between deep motivational systems and executive control structures is fundamental to how we engage with the world in a flexible, organized, and future-oriented manner (Panksepp, 1998a, 1998b, 2003, 2005a, 2005b, 2006a, 2006b; Panksepp & Biven, 2012).

Continuum of SEEKING Expression

Panksepp found that the SEEKING system does not operate in binary terms. It is not simply "on" or "off". Rather, it functions along a continuum, ranging from healthy, adaptive engagement to dysregulated states that can be either underactive or overactive. This spectrum of expression is shaped by neurobiological factors, developmental experiences, and the demands of the environment. Table 6.1 proposes a practical and somewhat observable continuum of the expression of SEEKING in humans.

At optimal levels of activation, the SEEKING system supports what we might call "engagement". In this state, an individual is alert, energized, and motivated to interact with the world. There is a sense of intrinsic interest in one's surroundings, and behavior is organized toward meaningful exploration. This state is marked by healthy dopaminergic tone in the mesolimbic and mesocortical pathways, particularly between the VTA, nucleus accumbens, and medial prefrontal cortex. These neural circuits promote persistence, flexibility, and anticipation.

As activation intensifies, particularly in novel or highly stimulating contexts, SEEKING can become heightened. This is often adaptive manifesting as intense curiosity, problem-solving,

Table 6.1 Continuum of SEEKING Expression

Level	Description	Neural Correlates	Neurochemicals	Functional Role
1. Healthy Curiosity	Adaptive motivation and interest in the environment; curiosity, engagement, and spontaneous play	Balanced activation of the mesolimbic dopamine pathway; VTA to nucleus accumbens and PFC	Dopamine (moderate), glutamate, endogenous opioids	Promotes learning, creativity, and engagement; supports psychological vitality
2. Energized Exploration	High but still regulated drive toward novelty, problem-solving, and goal pursuit	Heightened activation of VTA, nucleus accumbens, lateral hypothalamus, and medial forebrain bundle	Elevated dopamine, orexin, moderate endogenous opioids	Facilitates focused action and innovation; fuels goal achievement
3. Hyper-SEEKING/ Mania	Overactivation of SEEKING resulting in manic energy, impulsivity, and unrealistic goal setting	Overactive dopaminergic signaling, reduced top-down regulation from prefrontal cortex	Excessive dopamine, low serotonin, reduced GABA inhibition	Can lead to risk-taking, overcommitment, emotional dysregulation
4. Blunted SEEKING/ Apathy	Underactivation of SEEKING; characterized by lethargy, lack of motivation, or depressive withdrawal	Hypoactivity in VTA and nucleus accumbens; reduced PFC engagement	Low dopamine, low norepinephrine, altered serotonin	Limits adaptability, reduces quality of life, impairs resilience

Level	Description	Neural Correlates	Neurochemicals	Functional Role
5. Pathological Misdirection (e.g. Addiction)	SEEKING becomes hijacked by narrow or maladaptive targets (e.g. substances, compulsive behaviors)	Dysregulated mesolimbic dopamine circuits; hijacking of SEEKING by cue-induced striatal activity	High dopamine spikes in response to specific cues, low tonic dopamine elsewhere	Sustains compulsive cycles at the expense of broader adaptive functioning

innovation, or creative insight. However, when this arousal becomes excessive or disconnected from meaningful outcomes, SEEKING may shift into compulsive or perseverative behavior. In such cases, the individual may engage in repetitive activities, excessive novelty-seeking, or addictive patterns, reflecting hyperdopaminergic states or disrupted prefrontal modulation.

At the other end of the spectrum lies the underactive expression of SEEKING. Here, dopaminergic signaling is reduced, particularly in the prefrontal-limbic circuitry. The individual may present with apathy, anhedonia, lack of initiative, or disengagement from the external world. This blunted state is frequently observed in depressive disorders, negative symptoms of schizophrenia, or in certain neurodegenerative conditions. It may also emerge in the aftermath of trauma or prolonged helplessness, where the SEEKING system has been chronically suppressed or dysregulated.

Throughout the continuum, the functional role of SEEKING remains the same to mobilize the organism toward adaptive engagement with its environment. What changes is the regulation of this drive and how well it is modulated by experience, executive function, and affective context. Healthy SEEKING promotes learning, resilience, and purposeful activity. Dysregulated SEEKING, in either direction, undermines the capacity for goal-directed living and impairs the sense of agency. It is important to remember that SEEKING, like all emotions, is culture bound and may be expressed differently depending on the individual's socioeconomic status, sex, gender, racial, ethnic, ableness, and other cultural factors.

Practical Translation of SEEKING

The hardest part of teaching clients about the SEEKING system is that essentially no one outside the academic/scientific community recognizes it as a distinct emotional system that is a tool for living. Paradigm shifts are hard enough when we are trying to reorient our clients into thinking that there are only seven basic biological emotions that are built-in tools for survival. However, in this case, we are introducing a brand-new construct and the wonderful gifts that SEEKING brings to our human experience. It will not be hard for most to understand how SEEKING is strongly related to addictions. It makes intuitive sense. On the other hand, how do we translate the positive and adaptive characteristics into everyday life?

There is a core part of your brain, something built into your biology, that is designed to help you move through the world with energy, curiosity, and purpose. This system is not something you had to learn; it is something you were born with. It is called the SEEKING system, and it comes from deep in the brain, in areas that evolved long before language or logic. All mammals have it. It drives us to explore, to pursue what we need, and to engage with life even when we do not yet know what we are looking for.

The SEEKING system is fueled by a specific brain chemical called dopamine, that acts like a signal that something "out there" might be important or rewarding. This system becomes active when you are looking forward to something, trying to solve a problem, making plans, or simply following a sense of interest. It is not about finishing things; it is about the drive to begin. It is the biological foundation for motivation, engagement, and hope.

From a survival standpoint, this system evolved to help us find food, shelter, and social contact. But in humans, it became more complex as it helps us pursue meaning, relationships, creativity, and growth. When this system is functioning well, people tend to feel alive, motivated, and curious. They want to learn. They are able to imagine possibilities. But after trauma or chronic stress, the SEEKING system can go quiet. Biologically, this makes sense. The brain shifts into protective survival modes such as fight, flight, or freeze and shuts down systems that are not essential for immediate safety. Over time, if that shutdown persists, people may feel numb, lost, or like they no longer care about things that once mattered. This is not a character flaw. It is a biological adaptation to threat. The SEEKING system has not disappeared: it has been put on hold.

The practical advantage of understanding this is that we can begin to reactivate the SEEKING system not through force or pressure, but through gentle stimulation. Activities that are new, meaningful, or even slightly unfamiliar can begin to signal to your brain that it is safe enough to explore again. This might be as simple as taking a new route home, trying a creative hobby, reading something that sparks interest, or imagining future goals without pressure to achieve them right away.

In counseling, we often focus on helping the brain recognize that it is no longer in a state of emergency. As that happens, the SEEKING system begins to come back online. Clients often describe feeling "more like themselves", or noticing that they are interested in things again. That is not just psychological it is neurobiological. It is your brain returning to its natural rhythm of engagement with the world. When we support the SEEKING system, we are not just encouraging activity. We are helping restore the biological basis for hope, agency, and emotional aliveness. Remember, the SEEKING system does not require you to know exactly where you are going. It just needs you to move toward something that feels even slightly meaningful or new.

Counseling Goals for SEEKING (Neurobiological Perspective)

Goal: To support the client in reactivating curiosity, motivation, and forward momentum by strengthening the SEEKING system's connection to purposeful action, emotional vitality, and adaptive engagement with the world.

Rationale: The SEEKING system is the foundation of exploratory behavior, intrinsic motivation, and the emotional tone of "wanting". It drives the organism to learn, discover, problem-solve, and pursue goals. Neurochemically, the SEEKING system is powered primarily by dopamine, which fuels the anticipatory aspects of reward and sustained goal-directed activity.

Neuroanatomically, SEEKING is rooted in the VTA, nucleus accumbens, MFB, and prefrontal cortex. These circuits coordinate exploratory behavior and cognitive flexibility. When dysregulated, SEEKING can present as apathy, helplessness, indecision, or anhedonia.

Alternatively, in manic or compulsive states, SEEKING may become overactive and detached from reflective control.

Clinical Application: In therapy, the goal is to help the client recognize where their SEEKING energy is alive, where it has been blocked, and how it can be safely re-engaged. Clients who have experienced trauma, chronic stress, depression, or oppressive environments often learn to shut down the SEEKING system to preserve safety or conserve energy. This can lead to emotional flatness, reduced initiative, or a loss of direction.

Counseling interventions might involve helping clients set small, meaningful goals, engage in curiosity-driven tasks, or identify patterns of anticipation and motivation in their lives. Even playful experimentation, sensory exploration, and imagining future scenarios can help reawaken SEEKING.

Ultimately, the therapeutic aim is to affirm that the client's inner drive is not broken and it may simply be dormant, cautious, or misdirected. By reconnecting to the SEEKING system, clients regain a sense of agency, vitality, and creative problem-solving. This system is central to resilience and recovery and it helps us feel alive and capable of moving forward.

Here are some general points that the counselor (and educational and family members) might want to keep in mind when working with a client on the SEEKING system:

Therapeutic Touchpoints/Goals for SEEKING in the Affective Inventory Framework

The ideas the client should walk away with:

1 SEEKING Is the Brain's Curiosity and Motivation System; It Drives Exploration and Growth
SEEKING is a biologically rooted emotional system that energizes us to pursue novelty, solve problems, and engage with the world. It is what makes us feel eager, focused, and intrinsically motivated. This system underlies all goal-directed behavior from learning to walking, from imagining the future to making a plan.

2 Arousal, Anticipation, and Engagement Are Signs That the SEEKING System Is Active
When people feel curious, driven, or "in the zone", the SEEKING system is firing. It generates a sense of purpose and forward movement. This system does not wait for a reward, it is reward in itself. Dopamine is released in anticipation of action, not just upon success, which means activation itself is therapeutic and enlivening.

3 The SEEKING System Is Essential for Learning and Neuroplasticity
Dopamine-driven exploration helps forge new neural connections and keeps the brain flexible. When people feel interested or motivated, their brain is primed for growth and change. In therapy, activating SEEKING supports insight, behavioral experimentation, and cognitive reorganization. It is the emotional foundation of learning and recovery.

4 Depression, Trauma, and Chronic Stress Can Shut Down SEEKING
When individuals are exposed to ongoing adversity, unpredictability, or helplessness, the SEEKING system can go offline. This looks like apathy, lack of interest, hopelessness, or an inability to initiate. This shutdown is not laziness but neurobiological exhaustion. Therapy should focus on gently reawakening SEEKING through small wins, novelty, and relational encouragement.

5 SEEKING Is Directional but Not Specific: It Needs Structure to Thrive
The SEEKING system provides energy and drive, but it needs clear, emotionally safe goals to organize that energy. Without direction, SEEKING may become restless, anxious, or even obsessive. Helping clients clarify values, visualize positive futures, and set manageable goals gives the system something constructive to pursue.

6 Imagination and Creativity Are Core Expressions of SEEKING
Daydreaming, fantasizing, and imagining alternative futures are not distractions; they are core expressions of an active SEEKING system. These behaviors allow the brain to simulate possible realities and rehearse adaptive responses. Therapy can validate these tendencies as strengths, especially in clients who have survived by escaping inward.
7 SEEKING Is Reinforced by Safe Challenge and Relational Support
The SEEKING system is most productive when people feel supported, not overwhelmed. Safe risks, playful experimentation, and enthusiastic feedback from others help sustain engagement. Whether a child solving a puzzle or an adult trying a new skill, motivation flourishes in a context of emotional safety and encouragement.
8 Substance Use and Behavioral Addictions Can Hijack the SEEKING System
Drugs, compulsive behaviors, and maladaptive risk-taking often exploit the brain's dopamine-based SEEKING circuitry. These behaviors mimic the reward anticipation of SEEKING but offer little real growth or connection. Therapy should help clients identify genuine sources of meaning and exploration that restore the integrity of this system.
9 Clients Deserve to Feel Excited About Life Again
Many clients have learned to suppress or mistrust their own curiosity. They may have been punished for asking questions, discouraged from dreaming, or worn down by failure. Reclaiming SEEKING means rediscovering what feels energizing, satisfying, and hopeful. Therapy should help clients connect with what lights them up inside, and then pursue it.
10 SEEKING Is the Drive Toward Possibility: It Is the Engine of Healing
At its core, SEEKING is about possibility: the belief that something new, better, or more meaningful is out there. In this way, SEEKING is a powerful therapeutic ally. When we activate SEEKING, we activate the part of the brain that believes change is possible and wants to move toward it.

Another resource is added here to assist with translating the SEEKING system beyond the counseling office. The client handout (Client Handout 1) can be for the client to take home as a reminder about how to incorporate SEEKING into their everyday thinking and actions. It has been included here for easy reference but also to help the reader understand how the Therapeutic Touchpoints can be extended into client homework.

Client Handout 1: The SEEKING System: Your Brain's Curiosity and Motivation Engine

Client Handout 1: SEEKING	Description
What Is SEEKING?	Your brain's "go-get-it" system. It makes you curious, excited to try new things, and motivated to explore and grow
How Can I Tell It Is On?	You feel eager, focused, and interested just like when you can't wait to start a project or figure something out. That "spark" is SEEKING
Why Is It So Important?	When SEEKING is active, your brain is ready to learn, grow, and try new things. It builds new brain connections and helps you change for the better
What Turns It Off?	Feeling sad, stuck, scared, or overwhelmed. These emotions can temporarily shut SEEKING down to help you conserve energy. It is your brain's way of protecting you
How Do We Turn It Back On?	Start small. Try something new, even if It is tiny. Ask questions. Play. Get support from people who believe in you
Is Imagination Part of SEEKING?	Yes! Daydreaming, drawing, pretending, and wondering about the future are all ways your brain uses SEEKING to imagine new possibilities
What Helps It Work Best?	Feeling safe, supported, and encouraged not pressured. Fun challenges and curiosity-friendly environments grow SEEKING
Can It Get Tricked?	Yes. Substances or risky behaviors can hijack SEEKING by giving fake rewards without true fulfillment or growth
What If I've Lost It?	You can get it back. SEEKING can go quiet during stress or depression, but curiosity and motivation return with safety, support, and small steps
Why Does It Matter in Counseling?	SEEKING is the part of you that believes life can get better and wants to go find out how. In therapy, we help that part wake up again

In addition, here are some ideas for questions that can help the client incorporate the ideas about the emotion into their everyday life:

Client Reflection Questions:

1 When do you feel most curious or excited to explore something new?

2 What's one small activity that makes you feel energized or hopeful?

3 Describe a time when you used your imagination to solve a problem or feel better.

4 Who helps you feel safe and supported when trying new things?

5 What's one goal you'd like to work toward using your SEEKING energy?

Note: A downloadable version of this handout is available via the webpage for the book at: www.routledge.com/9781041250135

References

Davis, K., & Montag, C. (2019). Selected principles of Pankseppian affective neuroscience. *Frontiers in Neuroscience*, 12(1025), 1–10.

Panksepp, J. (1998a). *Affective neuroscience: The foundations of human and animal emotions*. Oxford University Press.

Panksepp, J. (1998b). The periconscious substrates of consciousness: Affective states and the evolutionary origins of the SELF. *Journal of Consciousness Studies*, 5(5–6), 566–582.

Panksepp, J. (2003). At the interface between the affective, behavioral, and cognitive neurosciences: Decoding the emotional feelings of the brain. *Brain and Cognition*, 52(1), 4–14.

Panksepp, J. (2005a). Affective consciousness: Core emotional feelings in animals and humans. *Consciousness and Cognition*, 14(1), 30–80.

Panksepp, J. (2005b). On the embodied neural nature of the core emotional affects. *Journal of Consciousness Studies*, 12(8–10), 158–184.

Panksepp, J. (2006a). Emotional endophenotypes in evolutionary psychiatry. *Progress in Neuro-Psychopharmacology & Biological Psychiatry*, 30(5), 774–784.

Panksepp, J. (2006b). The core emotional systems of the mammalian brain: The fundamental substrates of human emotions. In H. Corrigall, H. Payne, & I. Wilkinson (Eds.), *About a body: Working with the embodied mind in psychotherapy* (pp. 14–32). Routledge.

Panksepp, J., & Biven, L. (2012). *The archaeology of mind: Neuroevolutionary origins of human emotions*. W. W. Norton.

Chapter 7

RAGE/ANGER

Note: The label of RAGE/ANGER will be represented from now on with the common term of ANGER. This is a more generic term that might better traverse the continuum of the emotion and is probably more child friendly. However, the clinician should use the term that is best suited to the client.

Allostatic Function of ANGER

The allostatic purpose of ANGER (RAGE) is to establish and protect physical and social boundaries preferably without causing harm to the physical self or others, or damaging self-interests. It is a structured, goal-directed response rooted in survival. While it is an energizing emotion, it does not feel good for the most part! Although, sometimes exerting the energy of anger is empowering and that can feel more positive albeit complicated. Anger is simply about exerting protective energy to bring about useful change.

Anger is a wonderful energy, it is powerful, targeted, exciting, raw, sophisticated, surgical, painful, exaggerated, sometimes destructive, and is the emotion that has your back when you are in a tight spot and need to defend. It is a fundamental neural circuit that prepares the organism to defend itself, resist interference, or respond to perceived injustice (Berkowitz, 1989; Panksepp & Biven, 2012). It originates in subcortical motor and affective systems but is shaped and regulated by frontal cortical networks (Craig, 2009; Grecucci et al., 2024; Harmon-Jones & Peterson, 2009). Its activation produces a powerful state of emotional arousal, organized around the imperative to push back, assert boundaries, or restore agency in the face of threat or frustration.

Physiology and Neuroanatomical Features of ANGER

The sympathetic nervous system is activated during anger and so heart rate increases, blood pressure goes up, neurotransmitter such as norepinephrine increases, cortisol is elevated, adrenaline elevates to increase physical readiness and increases in respiration and muscle tension can occur (Gregg & Siegel, 2001; Kolb & Whishaw, 2020). Males tend to have higher

DOI: 10.4324/9781003745686-9

testosterone-linked aggression, and some studies have indicated that females tend to have greater or variable cortisol sensitivity during relational anger (Denson et al., 2018; Manfredi, 2024). A detailed analyses of biopsychosocial sex differences in ANGER is beyond the scope of this work. However, there is much available on the subject albeit no single source covering the entire subject. Hopefully, in the future we will see a codified set of publications that can guide clinical work.

Panksepp (1998a, 1998b, 2003, 2005a, 2005b, 2006a, 2006b; Panksepp & Biven, 2012) found that the ANGER system originates in deep, evolutionarily conserved regions of the brain. Its core circuitry lies in the medial and periaqueductal gray (PAG) of the midbrain and extends into the medial hypothalamus and amygdala, with critical involvement of the bed nucleus of the stria terminalis and PAG. Electrical stimulation of these areas in animals reliably produces affectively intense, coordinated aggressive behaviors (snarling, growling, striking) accompanied by a subjective experience of anger or fury when translated to human emotional life.

Neurochemically, the ANGER system is driven by glutamatergic excitation, substance P, and corticotropin-releasing factor, and is modulated by low serotonin levels, which reduce inhibitory control and increase the likelihood of reactive aggression. Testosterone and norepinephrine also influence the system's responsiveness, particularly under conditions of perceived threat or social challenge.

The amygdala plays a dual role in the ANGER system. While traditionally associated with fear, it also contributes to aggressive motivation when certain inputs converge, particularly when fear and frustration are paired with a sense of social defeat or physical restraint. In such cases, the amygdala activates hypothalamic and brainstem circuits that prepare the body for attack or resistance (Kolb & Whishaw, 2020).

Frontal cortical areas, especially the orbitofrontal cortex and anterior cingulate cortex, are essential for modulating this system (Craig, 2009; Grecucci et al., 2024). These regions exert top-down inhibition, allowing the organism to assess context, inhibit impulsive outbursts, and choose more adaptive responses when aggression is not appropriate. When these cortical areas are damaged, underdeveloped, or functionally dysregulated as seen in some forms of traumatic brain injury, impulsivity disorders, or early developmental trauma, ANGER system activation may become disinhibited and excessive (Blair, 2016).

Cultural Factors

Culturally, the social acceptability of anger varies dramatically. In some societies, anger is viewed as a legitimate and even necessary expression of autonomy or boundary protection, particularly for boys and men. In others, anger is considered disruptive or dangerous, especially when expressed by women or children (Manfredi, 2024). These beliefs influence not only behavioral norms but also the development of the neural pathways involved in emotion regulation. Children who are shamed, punished, or ignored for expressing anger may internalize the message that this feeling is unsafe, which can result in suppressed emotional expression or somatization. Alternatively, children raised in environments where anger is modeled as uncontrolled or aggressive may overexpress it, without learning to channel it adaptively.

Gender expectations further complicate the neuropsychological expression of anger. Boys are often socialized to express anger more freely, while girls may be socialized to transform their anger into sadness, anxiety, or people-pleasing behavior. These patterns are not merely social, they become inscribed in the nervous system. Repeated experiences of suppression or invalidation alter the limbic-prefrontal balance, often leading to diminished top-down regulation of emotional arousal (Craig, 2009; Grecucci et al., 2024). Conversely, excessive inhibitory control that disconnects the individual from their own emotional cues, in other words, continued subjugation of the expression of anger creates a lack of agency that is very difficult to undo.

Developmental trauma can also fundamentally alter the brain's anger circuitry. When children are exposed to chronic stress, neglect, or abuse, the ANGER system may become hypersensitive, leading to impulsive aggression, mood dysregulation, or hypervigilance. In such cases, the prefrontal cortex often fails to effectively regulate subcortical activation, and the child may struggle to differentiate between perceived and actual threats. Conversely, children who have never been permitted to express anger may develop an underactive or fragmented sense of self-protection and assertiveness, which can manifest in depression, passivity, or difficulty setting boundaries (Kolb & Whishaw, 2020).

As clinicians and educators, we must assess not only the frequency or intensity of a child's anger but also the relational, cultural, and neurobiological scaffolding around it. Has the child been given tools to recognize, name, and express anger constructively? Has their anger been punished, ignored, or dismissed? Have they seen models of regulated, values-driven assertiveness, or have they only known anger as either explosive or forbidden? These questions guide us toward a more compassionate and culturally competent approach to supporting children in their emotional development.

Continuum of ANGER Expression: Assertiveness to Physical Rage

As with all emotions, anger can be evoked top-down or bottom-up depending on the severity and immediacy of the moment. From a top-down perspective, in its early stages, the ANGER system is primed by conscious frustration: a blocked goal, an unfair treatment, or an encroaching threat. That moment of friction activates the medial amygdala and hypothalamus, that detect possible novel threat and preparing the body for a reactive surge. As tension builds, signals descend into the PAG, a midbrain hub that transforms rising emotion into potential action (Panksepp & Biven, 2012). From a bottom-up perspective, these deeper areas fire first when the threat is immediate and very dangerous to self or others. In this type of situation, the brain perceives the threat in a plain non-thinking sensory manner, the deeper brain regions activate instantly before the frontal and problem-solving systems can make sense of what is actually going on. It should be noted that when the prefrontal checks are immature or weakened by trauma, impulsivity, or chronic stress, the ANGER system is primed most of the time in a bottom-up way. The result is less conscious reflection and more impulsive reactions for these individuals.

The expression of anger operates along a neurobiologically supported continuum, where context, personality, and problem-solving thinking mechanisms determine whether anger serves adaptive purposes or escalates into harmful physical acts of rage. We are hard wired to feel anger and rage. There is nothing we can do to change this. It is our biology. However, for mammals and humans, we tend to survive better if we use our frontal systems to diplomatically navigate our way through difficult situations. The prefrontal cortex acts as a regulatory brake on subcortical anger (core emotion) in a top-down manner. It takes quite a bit of maturity and prefrontal energy to defend oneself by being assertive (the least energetic or abrasive expression of anger) as opposed to other more physical or loud forms of expression.

Babies are not born with fully formed frontal systems and we humans do not really reach full power in this area until our mid 20s (Kolb & Whishaw, 2020). Therefore, the nuances of assertiveness become online as executive functions develop. The wiring in our frontal systems is shaped by watching the modeling shown by our caregivers. Life experiences also challenge our systems as we take what we have learned about translating anger and apply it to new situations. Sometimes we have good results and sometimes we have no clue what happened except that we are now in a whole lot of trouble! This trial-and-error process happens all day and our frontal lobes come online more and more until the ANGER system ideally becomes a somewhat curated and wonderful life tool: Core affective power when we need it and nuances when we don't.

Table 7.1 offers a continuum of anger (ANGER) expression that might be helpful for us personally and for our clients. There are choices when it comes to evoking the ANGER system, and we need to hit our mark to get anger to work for us. Let's say that again. There are shades of anger, and we need to use them efficiently by exerting the least amount of energy to get what we want. Homeostasis and allostasis are achieved by the efficient use of resources. If the core emotion of anger is strong energy consuming resource, then it should be used wisely. It should not consume our energy resources any more than necessary because then we get tired and other more positive opportunities can pass us by.

Assertiveness is the least caustic form of anger on our health because it does not require massive physiological exertion or elevations in hormones, neurotransmitters and bodily systems that can reduce (in the long run) the integrity of our immune systems. Assertiveness is essentially a very economical way of dealing with boundary setting situations because the frontal (top) systems are maximized for being preemptive and predictive. They are trying to navigate the situation with the least amount of discord and the maximum amount of value. Assertiveness is a wonderful allostatic tool in that it conserves resources while moving the agenda forward. Assertiveness is also somewhat of an art form and is not always necessarily successful.

Sometimes anger is a slow boil, and life just becomes consistently irritating indicating that we have to change something because we are starting to have a quick trigger, our health is declining, or our relationships at home or work are starting to suffer. Anger is not a comfortable emotion and most of us do not like feeling it especially on a consistent basis. So, there is impetus for change, and this is our deep-self saying I don't want to feel this anymore and I need to look elsewhere for relief. It is a pearl in the oyster. Anger provides the energy for change.

You will notice that as the level of anger increases on the Table 7.1, the frontal systems start to decline in the ability to finesse what we want. By the time we get to anger and rage we see that the top-down communication is compromised, and so aggressive and violent impulses have few restraints. Aggression and violence are primal, non-thinking, and energetic ways of finding an outcome to an extreme situation. We need adrenaline to pump up the energy that is needed for the physical offense or defense. Adrenaline (epinephrine) is an interesting hormone and neurotransmitter. In extreme situations it activates for just a few minutes and is cleared from the body. However, the effects can last for hours if cortisol is released, or the individual has triggering thoughts later about the event. Residual feelings of anger can persist as emotional memory encoding happens for hours after or longer (LeDoux, 2000). So, while the overt physiology and conscious experience of anger may be gone quickly, there can be residual effects that keep the individual primed or on the lookout for the need for anger again. Survival and allostasis are operating here again. If we become angry to the point of adrenaline and cortisol release, then it means that we needed to do something quite powerful to protect our boundaries (or the safety of others). It makes sense that something of this level of import might happen again, and we will need the physical energy to prevent it from happening again, so it stays until we decide what to do next, or we are sure that the threat is not coming back.

It is important to remember that Anger, like all emotions, is culture bound and may be expressed differently depending on the individual's socioeconomic status, sex, gender, racial, ethnic, ableness, history, and other cultural factors.

Table 7.1 Continuum of ANGER Expression

Level of ANGER	Description	Neural Correlates	Functional Role
Assertiveness	Calm, confident expression of boundaries or needs	Prefrontal cortex (especially dorsolateral PFC), anterior cingulate cortex	Social boundary-setting, conflict resolution
Frustration	Initial, manageable irritation in response to blocked goals	Anterior insula, amygdala, ventromedial PFC	Motivation to change environment
Irritability	Heightened sensitivity to provocation, often chronic	Hyperactive amygdala, dysregulated serotoninergic pathways	Maladaptive in interpersonal contexts
Anger	Affective state with physiological arousal and action readiness	RAGE system (medial amygdala, hypothalamus, periaqueductal gray)	Mobilizes defensive behaviour–behavior
Aggression	Behavioral output of poorly regulated anger	Reduced top-down regulation from orbitofrontal cortex, enhanced limbic activity	Detrimental; linked to psychopathologies
Rage	Extreme, uncontrollable anger with intense arousal	Overactivation of RAGE circuitry, impaired cortical inhibition	Often destructive; associated with trauma/impulse

Practical Translation of ANGER

Speaking practically, and for those of us who work in schools, it is a familiar experience when we see a child sitting outside the Vice Principal's office first thing in the day after they have had a meltdown on the bus going to school that morning. We know that It is going to be a tough day! Perhaps what we are not aware of, is that this child's physiology is now primed to see threat throughout the day and/or have shaky frontal system control. While the event and the discipline are over at 8:15am (in the minds of the adults), the child has hours to go before physiological systems calm down. However, we expect the child to meet the academic and social demands of the day as if the physiological melt-down and residual chemicals have dissipated. Even if we have the opportunity to debrief with the child to gain top-down control over behavior/aggression at 8:15am, it still does not change the physiology for the rest of the day (McEwen, 2007: LeDoux, 2000; Southwick et al., 2005). For some students, going to class and a regular schedule might help them gain some sense of distraction, safety, predictability, and control. For others, especially those students with trauma backgrounds, it can mean the rest of the day is a waste as the biochemistry keeps on circling and infecting new events.

We tend to work with students in schools only when their behavior becomes the squeaky wheel. Their anger is displayed inappropriately, and something needs to be done. We try punishment, counseling, suspensions etc. but we do not plan for the physiology. When we see the student that is about to have a really bad day, we need to plan alternate strategies for helping them be aware of their physiological sensitivity and have skills to self-soothe and get back on track.

Most of the time, the student gets the message that anger is wrong, bad, banned or something that does not belong in school. We confuse the emotion with the expression of extreme maladaptive behavior and the message that we send to students is that anger is bad, period. This message is very powerful and very destructive to a developing child because we are telling them that when they are angry, *they* are bad. The message should be something like:

> Yes! defend yourself! Yes! create boundaries! There are lots of ways to do this and let's learn and practice them together! We support you having agency! So, don't stop getting angry, let's just find ways you can express well. Remember that the chemicals will stay with you for a while so be kind to yourself and try not to react quickly today, try to give yourself some time to get over this. That way you get what you want, and you don't get into more trouble before you have fixed what just happened.

The best way to help our students is to first help them identify when they are angry because children don't automatically know. Then, help them automatically switch to thinking about what they want to do about the emotion. They need to know they have options. Options are prefrontal cortex thoughts that begin the top-down translation of emotion into action.

The ANGER system has a social logic. It is what powers boundary-setting, resistance to coercion, and the indignation we feel at injustice. Anger, in this frame, becomes a force of personal agency. When modulated, it fuels assertiveness, motivates resistance to harm, and draws lines in relational sand.

It is best if the counselor and the client define the power of anger together. (Please notice that I did not use the term "control anger" here). The power of anger keeps the positive in mind and we need to do that as much as possible in a world where we constantly infer that "if you show anger, you are a bad person". This can be done by creating a plan for anger going forward, discussing events that evoke anger and how to handle them, drawing pictures and cartoons to help map out the sequence of events, or making lists of people to go to for advice. It is also advisable to repeatedly give the message that anger is good (even if it feels bad) because the client has been living in a world where the message is negative (anger is always bad), and the paradigm shift has not yet occurred. As long as we are imparting a sense of agency about anger, then we are doing the right thing. When you take away anger, you take away agency. And why would anyone who wants respect from self and others voluntarily give up this precious emotion? or could they even if they wanted to? So, let us think of anger-agency as synonyms. Let's always have that hyphen in there...anger-agency. As a counselor ask yourself "Is this anger a call to protect? What are they protecting? Why did they have to use so much energy? Or is this anger a chemical residue of a previous angry encounter?" The Table 7.1 for the Continuum of Anger Expression might be a good reference point to share with the client. It is even *more* powerful if you and the client create a personal table where the client uses their own words and pictures to chart their journey of different levels of anger and what options could be available at each level of anger arousal.

Counseling Goal for ANGER (Neurobiological Perspective)

Goal: To support the client in identifying early signs of escalating anger and safely channeling intense emotional energy by enhancing interoceptive awareness, restoring regulatory pathways, and strengthening executive control over reactive motor patterns.

Rationale: From a neurochemical perspective, the ANGER system is energized by a surge of excitatory neurotransmitters, particularly substance P, glutamate, and elevated levels of dopamine (Panksepp & Biven, 2012). This creates a cascade of motor readiness and reactive energy intended for defense or protest. When unregulated, this system can override reasoning and impulse control, especially in developing or dysregulated brains.

Neuroanatomically, ANGER is coordinated through the medial amygdala, hypothalamus, and dorsal PAG, all of which trigger high-arousal responses. These subcortical regions are often activated before the prefrontal cortex can assess context or consequences. In clients with chronic irritability or explosive anger, the orbitofrontal cortex and ventromedial prefrontal cortex, which are responsible for inhibiting impulsive actions, may be underactive or underdeveloped.

Clinical Application: The counseling goal is to guide the client toward understanding how anger arises in the body (often with heat, pressure, or restlessness) and to help them find ways to name, move, or redirect the energy in constructive ways. This might involve structured physical outlets, somatic tracking, or visual mapping of anger cues. As insight grows, the focus shifts to strengthening top-down regulation through body–mind practices, reflective questioning, and co-regulation within safe relationships. Ultimately, the goal is not to suppress anger, but to restore its original purpose while making space for more adaptive expression.

Therapeutic Touchpoints/Goals for ANGER in the Affective Inventory Framework

The ideas the client should walk away with:

1 ANGER Is the Brain's Protest and Boundary System: It Signals Violation, Not Violence
The ANGER system evolved to help us protect ourselves when our needs, boundaries, or safety are threatened. It activates when we are blocked, restrained, treated unfairly, or exposed to chronic frustration. Anger is not inherently destructive because it is a form of emotional protest that says, "Something is not okay".

2 Anger Is Often a Cover for Pain, Powerlessness, or Shame
ANGER can be a secondary response that rises to defend more vulnerable emotional states like hurt, fear, or abandonment. In individuals with trauma histories, anger may be the only emotion they feel safe expressing. Therapy can help clients explore what lies beneath the anger and teach them how to express it without harm or withdrawal.

3 ANGER Is Fast, Physical, and Difficult to Inhibit: This Is By Design
The ANGER system activates subcortically in regions like the PAG and medial hypothalamus, bypassing conscious reasoning to enable fast defense. This is why angry reactions often feel automatic and overwhelming. Helping clients understand this reduces shame and opens the door to learning regulation, not repression.

4 Chronic Suppression of ANGER Leads to Shutdown, Somatization, or Depression
When anger is repeatedly stifled or punished, especially in childhood, it doesn't disappear. It often turns inward, manifesting as chronic fatigue, physical tension, self-hatred, or depressive collapse. Restoring the ANGER system's healthy function means learning to recognize, name, and use anger as a source of strength, not a threat.

5 Explosive or Misplaced ANGER Often Signals a Nervous System on High Alert
For trauma survivors or neurodivergent individuals, the threshold for frustration may be much lower due to chronic nervous system dysregulation. What looks like an overreaction is often a reasonable reaction to accumulated, unspoken stress. Therapy should prioritize safety, emotional literacy, and titrated expression.

6 ANGER Without Skills Becomes Destructive: ANGER with Skills Becomes Power
Clients must learn to notice early signs of anger (tight jaw, clenched fists, shallow breath) and develop strategies for safe expression: grounding, movement, assertive communication, creative outlets. Healthy ANGER empowers self-protection, boundary setting, and advocacy not aggression.

7 ANGER Is a Sign That Something Needs to Change, Not That the Person Is "Bad"
When a child lashes out, when a teen slams a door, or when an adult explodes after being ignored, these are not just behavioral issues, they are emotional alarms. Therapy should help identify the unmet need or violated boundary beneath the anger and teach how to respond without harm to self or others.

8 Cultural and Familial Messages Shape How ANGER Is Expressed or Silenced
Many people were taught that anger is dangerous or unacceptable. Others were modeled explosive, unsafe expressions of ANGER. Therapy should explore how ANGER was learned, punished, or weaponized and begin the work of rewriting the narrative.

9 Movement, Voice, and Creativity Are Key Tools for Releasing ANGER Safely
Because ANGER is visceral and somatic, regulation must happen through the body and not just through talking. Exploring appropriate ways to deal with the energy are essential. Clients should be encouraged to *move* the energy, not suppress it.

10 ANGER When Integrated, Becomes a Source of Personal Power and Justice. Integrated anger becomes the voice that says "no" to abuse, exploitation, or invisibility. It allows clients to assert their needs, take up space, and advocate for fairness. It is the fire that fuels transformation both personally and collectively. The goal in therapy is not to eliminate ANGER, but to reclaim it as an agent of truth and boundary.

Client Handout 2: The ANGER System: Your Brain's Built-In Protector

Client Handout 2: ANGER	Description
What Is ANGER?	It is your brain's "stand-up-for-yourself" system. It shows up when something feels unfair, when you're blocked, or when you need to protect yourself
How Can I Tell It Is On?	You might feel hot, tight, jumpy, or ready to yell. You might clench your fists or feel like hitting or running. That's your body getting ready to act
Why Is It So Important?	ANGER helps protect your boundaries and gives you strength. When handled well, it helps you speak up and fix problems. It becomes trouble *only* when it hurts someone else or you
What Turns It Up Too High?	Feeling trapped, ignored, or not safe can make ANGER come on fast. It is not about being "bad" it is your brain trying to defend you
How Can We Calm It Down?	Breathe slow. Take a break. Move your body in a safe way. Talk to someone who can help. Learning to notice it early helps you stay in charge
Is Anger Always Bad?	No! Feeling ANGER means something matters to you. The goal is not to get rid of it, but to use it in a helpful way. It is a powerful tool for change
What Helps It Work Best?	Clear rules, feeling heard, safe outlets for energy, and knowing It is okay to talk about ANGER feelings. Respect plus boundaries = control
Can It Be Misused?	Yes. Sometimes people use their anger in ways that hurt others or themselves. Learning how to pause and express ANGER safely is the goal
What If I'm Scared of My Anger?	That's okay. Anger can feel big and scary. But with support, you can learn to understand it and use it to make good choices
Why Does It Matter in Counseling?	ANGER is a part of you that says: "This isn't okay". In therapy, we learn how to listen to that part, stay safe, and find strong, respectful ways to respond

In addition, here are some ideas for questions that can help the client incorporate the ideas about the emotion into their everyday life:

Client Reflection Handout: My ANGER System

1 What kinds of things make you feel angry or frustrated?

2 What does your body feel like when ANGER is turned on?

3 What's something that helps you calm down or take a break?

4 Who helps you feel safe when you're angry?

5 What's one way you can use your ANGER energy in a helpful way?

Draw Your ANGRY Self!
Use the space below to draw what your ANGER system looks like when It is turned on. You can draw yourself being angry in a safe way, calming yourself down, or turning your anger into something that will protect you.

Note: A downloadable version of this handout is available via the webpage for the book at: www.routledge.com/9781041250135

References

Berkowitz, L. (1989). Frustration-aggression hypothesis: Examination and reformulation. *Psychological Bulletin*, 106(1), 59–73.
Blair, R. J. R. (2016). The neurobiology of impulsive aggression. *Journal of Child Psychology and Psychiatry*, 57(3), 512–525.
Craig, A. D. (2009). How do you feel—now? The anterior insula and human awareness. *Nature Reviews Neuroscience*, 10(1), 59–70.
Denson, T., O'Dean, S., Blake, K., & Beames, J. (2018). Aggression in women: Behavior, brain and hormones. *Frontiers in Behavioral Neuroscience*, 12(81), 1–20.
Grecucci, A., Graci, F., Munari, E., Xiaoping, Yi, Salvato,G., & Messina, I. (2024). A fronto-insular network underlies individual variations in anger expression and control. *Imaging Neuroscience*, 2, imag-2-00348.
Gregg, T. R., & Siegel, A. (2001). Brain structures and neurotransmitters regulating aggression in cats: Implications for human aggression. *Progress in Neuro-Psychopharmacology & Biological Psychiatry*, 25(1), 91–140.
Harmon-Jones, E., & Peterson, C. K. (2009). Anger and frontal brain activity: EEG asymmetry consistent with approach motivation despite negative affective valence. *Journal of Personality and Social Psychology*, 74(3), 135–143.
Kolb, B., & Whishaw, I. (20
020). *Fundamentals of human neuroscience* (8th ed.). Worth.
LeDoux, J. E. (2000). Emotion circuits in the brain. *Annual Review of Neuroscience*, 23, 155–1 84. https://doi.org/10.1146/annurev.neuro.23.1.155
Panksepp, J. (1998a). *Affective neuroscience: The foundations of human and animal emotions.* Oxford University Press.
Panksepp, J. (1998b). The periconscious substrates of consciousness: Affective states and the evolutionary origins of the SELF. *Journal of Consciousness Studies*, 5(5–6), 566–582.
Panksepp, J. (2003). At the interface between the affective, behavioral, and cognitive neurosciences: Decoding the emotional feelings of the brain. *Brain and Cognition*, 52(1), 4–14.
Panksepp, J. (2005a). Affective consciousness: Core emotional feelings in animals and humans. *Consciousness and Cognition*, 14(1), 30–80.
Panksepp, J. (2005b). On the embodied neural nature of the core emotional affects. *Journal of Consciousness Studies*, 12(8–10), 158–184.
Panksepp, J. (2006a). Emotional endophenotypes in evolutionary psychiatry. *Progress in Neuro-Psychopharmacology & Biological Psychiatry*, 30(5), 774–784.
Panksepp, J. (2006b). The core emotional systems of the mammalian brain: The fundamental substrates of human emotions. In H. Corrigall, H. Payne, & I. Wilkinson (Eds.), *About a body: Working with the embodied mind in psychotherapy* (pp. 14–32). Routledge.
Panksepp, J., & Biven, L. (2012). *The archaeology of mind: Neuroevolutionary origins of human emotions.* W. W. Norton.
Manfredi, P. (2024). Basic affective systems and sex differences in the relationship between anger and fear. *International Journal of Environmental Research and Public Health*, 21(10), 1266.
McEwen, B. S. (2007). Physiology and neurobiology of stress and adaptation: Central role of the brain. *Physiological Reviews*, 87(3), 873–904.
Southwick, S. M., Vythilingam, M., & Charney, D. S. (2005). The psychobiology of depression and resilience to stress: Implications for prevention and treatment. *Annual Review of Clinical Psychology*, 1, 255–291.

Chapter 8

PLAY

Allostatic Function of PLAY

Play is not just a behavior. It is a biological drive, wired deep into the architecture of the mammalian brain. It is an essential core affect that is necessary for homeostasis and allostasis for two reasons: (1) it cements the social relationships with caregivers and social networks that protect us, and (2) it balances out the physiological and mental wear and tear of stress on the immune system. Play feels good! It energizes us. It is interesting. It is creative and without it, we are dull indeed. Dull does not contribute to survival or thriving or life satisfaction for mammals. Humans are always seeking opportunities and PLAY systems fuel the enjoyment of exploration. When PLAY is repressed, suppressed, or simply not present then that usually means that one or more of the other negative core emotions are overwhelming the system. Individuals with depression, for example, have little access to PLAY or to generate PLAY.

Physiological and Neuroanatomical Features of PLAY

PLAY triggers the release of a powerful cocktail of neurochemicals and hormones that promote social bonding, stress relief, learning, and joy. These biochemical responses are not incidental; they are central to why play is developmentally essential. In fact, Jaak Panksepp argued that PLAY is one of our primary emotional systems, and is as fundamental as FEAR, CARE, or SEEKING (Panksepp, 1998a, 1998b, 2003, 2005a, 2005b, 2006a, 2006b; Panksepp & Biven, 2012). What makes play unique is that it is essential for social development not just in childhood, but across the lifespan.

Panksepp's work started with observing young rats engaging in rough-and-tumble play. When they played, they vocalized with high-pitched chirps; something akin to laughter. But when they were isolated and deprived of play, the consequences were significant. Their ability to regulate emotions, form bonds, and navigate social cues became impaired. For Panksepp, this was compelling evidence that PLAY is not optional, it is developmentally necessary. It is the social glue that guides brain development and allostasis.

DOI: 10.4324/9781003745686-10

At the neural level, the PLAY system is coordinated by subcortical circuits, especially the periaqueductal gray (PAG), thalamus, basal ganglia, and cerebellum that are areas involved in movement, emotion, and instinctual behaviors. As children mature, higher brain regions like the prefrontal cortex start to shape how play is expressed, giving rise to imagination, rule-based games, and creative exploration.

PLAY activates the SEEKING and CARE systems in Jaak Panksepp's model, flooding the brain with dopamine and oxytocin (the love/cuddle neurohormone), reinforcing social connection, cooperative play, and curiosity. PLAY also boosts brain-derived neurotrophic factor for growth, which supports the growth and maintenance of neurons, especially in the hippocampus and prefrontal cortex. Sports play stimulates endorphins and adrenaline that contribute to euphoria, laughter, less pain, and more energy. On the other hand, quiet play environments lower cortisol, helping to buffer stress and trauma response which is especially important for neurodevelopment and mental health in children. Young children's cortisol levels decrease during safe and joyful play, and this is also supported by the calming effect of GABA (neurotransmitter) that helps with emotional regulation during play.

PLAY is not localized to a single brain region. Instead, it arises from dynamic interactions among motor systems, limbic affective circuits, reward pathways, and higher cortical regions. This hierarchical integration explains why play is so vital for emotional regulation, motor learning, executive development, social bonding, and creativity.

Continuum and Culture of PLAY Expression

Table 8.1 presents a neuropsychological and developmental model of PLAY, showing how it evolves from early sensorimotor experiences to complex intellectual play. Each stage is associated with specific brain regions, developmental periods, and behavioral features.

PLAY is not merely a luxury of childhood, it is a biologically embedded, evolutionarily conserved emotional system that plays a critical role in shaping the developing brain. From a neuropsychological perspective, the PLAY system, as described by Jaak Panksepp, is rooted in subcortical structures such as the PAG, dorsal thalamus, and basal ganglia. It is driven by a neurochemical foundation that includes endogenous opioids, dopamine, and oxytocin: all of which support joyful engagement, relational bonding, motor learning, and the regulation of affect. Although these neural circuits are universal across humans, their expression is profoundly influenced by the cultural context in which the child is raised.

Each culture establishes implicit and explicit guidelines regarding what forms of play are acceptable, encouraged, or discouraged. These cultural expectations shape not only behavior but also the development of neural pathways. In some communities, quiet, cooperative, or symbolic play is prioritized; in others, physical, loud, or risk-based play is more socially accepted. These norms affect how the prefrontal cortex modulates the innate subcortical drive to play. Cultural constraints or freedoms influence the degree to which the PLAY system is activated, reinforced, or inhibited. Gender socialization often adds another layer. Boys may receive more permission to engage in vigorous, exploratory play, while girls may be guided toward nurturing, imaginative, or verbal play patterns. These variations shape differential development across sensorimotor, emotional, and cognitive networks (Gray, 2013; Pellis & Pellis, 2009).

Socioeconomic conditions also influence the expression of the PLAY system. In resource-limited or high-stress environments, children may have limited access to safe, unstructured, developmentally appropriate play. The absence or restriction of play experiences affects key neurodevelopmental regions, including the prefrontal cortex, hippocampus, and cerebellum. These children may have fewer opportunities to build emotional flexibility, stress regulation, and prosocial behavior (Pellis & Pellis, 2009).

Table 8.1 Continuum of PLAY (Neuropsychological and Developmental Perspective)

Type of PLAY	Features	Developmental Stage	Neuropsychological Involvement	Examples
Sensorimotor Play	Bodily, repetitive, rhythmic movements	Infancy, early toddlerhood	Brainstem, cerebellum, basal ganglia	Rocking, spinning, mouthing objects
Rough-and-Tumble Play	Physical, social, unstructured	Toddlerhood through childhood	Periaqueductal gray, thalamus, motor cortex	Wrestling, chasing, mock fighting
Object/ Manipulative Play	Exploring and manipulating objects	Toddlerhood to adulthood	Parietal lobe, visual-motor areas	Stacking blocks, using tools
Social Play	Interactive, cooperative, sometimes competitive	Preschool years onward	Prefrontal cortex, social cognition networks	Hide-and-seek, team sports
Pretend/ Symbolic Play	Imaginative transformation of objects or roles	Ages 3+; peaks in early childhood	Temporal-parietal junction, medial PFC	Playing house, superhero games
Rule-Governed Play	Structured games with rules	School-age onward	Executive function regions, DLPFC	Board games, sports, video games
Creative/ Constructive Play	Artistic, building, or musical activities	All ages	Frontal and parietal lobes	Drawing, building, music improvisation
Narrative and Ritualized Play	Story-driven, emotionally expressive	Adolescence and adulthood	Default mode network, limbic system	Theater, cosplay, performance arts
Philosophical/ Intellectual Play	Mental experimentation, imaginative thinking	Adolescence through adulthood	Prefrontal cortex, theory of mind networks	Humor, abstract thinking

Educational priorities can further suppress natural play expression. In cultures that emphasize early academic achievement, young children may spend more time in structured instructional settings than engaging in free, creative, physical play. This premature academic emphasis limits access to the neurochemical benefits of play and may contribute to emotional blunting, social disconnection, or anxiety. When children are denied the opportunity to explore, imagine, and move freely, their PLAY system, and the associated development of emotional regulation and executive functioning, may be stunted (Panksepp & Biven, 2012).

In contrast, some cultures enrich and extend the PLAY system through intergenerational and ritual-based forms of play. In many Indigenous and traditional communities, play is infused with storytelling, rhythm, and relational practices that convey cultural values and emotional meaning. These experiences stimulate oxytocin release, support attachment security, and strengthen integration between emotion, memory, and social cognition (Kolb & Whishaw, 2020).

Therefore, in evaluating a child's emotional development and functioning, it is essential to ask: Has this child had access to play that reflects both their neurobiological needs and their cultural framework? Has the PLAY system been nurtured or suppressed? The answer to these questions has implications for emotional health, relational capacity, and developmental trajectory. Play is not an extracurricular activity. It is a neurodevelopmental requirement. Cultural context determines whether that need is honored or denied.

It is important to remember that PLAY, like all emotions, is culture bound and may be expressed differently depending on the individual's socioeconomic status, sex, gender, racial, ethnic, ableness, and other cultural factors.

Taken together, this body of research reveals that PLAY is more than just random fun. It is a biological need, a developmental engine, and a social teacher. Whether we are observing toddlers giggling in a sandbox, teenagers forming music bands in the garage, adults laughing with friends, or fans at football games, we are seeing a neural system at work that is building minds, sustaining creativity, and shaping relationships.

PLAY lays the groundwork for so many things we value such as empathy, social skills, emotional regulation, and executive functioning. It creates a safe space where young brains can rehearse the complexities of social life, test boundaries, learn cooperation, and build resilience. In adulthood, it sustains relationships, creates relationships, and fuels imagination and innovation.

We should watch children on the playground at school. It is pretty much an unstructured environment where we get to see how students negotiate social rules. Observing children from afar gives you the chance to see how they approach others, if they look for opportunities to laugh, are they leaders? Are they followers? Are they loners? They are supposed to play on the playground; given this expectation, what do they do with it?!

Sometimes, when I work with a student with the Affective Inventory, I think that my evaluation of how they express to PLAY is almost more important than assessing anything else. Why? First, it is a physiological core affect that promotes physical and mental health and without it, the student is much more likely to run into adjustment problems. Second, without the energizing brain and body chemicals that are released in PLAY I know that the student's worldview is dimmed and that it is much harder for them to meet the demands of everyday living. The lack of PLAY colors all things grey and decreases agency. They are out of balance and balance is the lifeblood of allostasis. Allostasis *is* agency and agency survives on us knowing that at all times we have flexible options to meet demands in life.

Most of the clients that I worked with in the neuropsychiatric hospital would be stumped when I would introduce them to PLAY in the Affective Inventory. In fact, after charting the six emotions in the Inventory, it would be very clear that the client had no clue how to generate play. Most of the time, they would see play as something that came to them from the outside in or randomly. They would win a lottery prize, or they would observe others playing games. All perceived it as an external locus of control. If play was not present in their lives it was because no one else had initiated it. Therefore, their access to the wonderful and enjoyable effects of dopamine, oxytocin, serotonin, and other PLAY chemicals was minimized. I came to see that as an outside agent, just even *talking* about PLAY while doing the Inventory changed our relationship and enhanced rapport. My job was to transform my outside influence into supporting the client owning their own PLAY system.

The Affective Inventory exercise for PLAY is a fun activity for both the counselor and the student. It explores joy and you will see the affect in the client brighten as you go through the inventory. It is joyful just to think about play and PLAY chemicals show themselves in the client's face, body, and attitude toward the activity. When you open up the world of opportunities for the child to consciously feel their body and brain–body during PLAY and then relate that to them being powerful and taking care of themselves and growing better brains, the world is so much more optimistic for them (and the SEEKING system is stimulated). You are helping them uncover the intrinsic agency that they innately possess to alter their everyday life at any time. Even during the hardest of times, it is ok to generate some play. In fact, it is necessary to have quick access to PLAY so that balance remains the taproot of allostasis.

Practical Translation of PLAY

In the beginning of working with this emotion, it might be helpful to talk with the individual about an understanding of what PLAY is and is not. Client Handout 3 is an example of a starter template for working with the child, or you can build a chart together. It is also very important for the child's caregivers to understand the nuances of PLAY. Sometimes, parents gain more than their child as they learn about the brain benefits of PLAY. They learn not only about themselves but also that they can help with instilling agency for PLAY in their child.

Can you have too much PLAY? Sure! You can have too much of any of the core emotions because they are tools for living but only if used wisely. Class clowns are full of PLAY but at the expense of focused learning in the classroom. Playing sports at the expense of academics is probably not good in the long run. As with any of the core affects, the goal is balance and allostasis and explorations into increasing PLAY should be couched in these terms. It is important to remember that PLAY, like all emotions, is culture bound and may be expressed differently depending on the individual's socioeconomic status, sex, gender, racial, ethnic, ableness, and other cultural factors.

Client Handout 3: PLAY Helps Your Brain Grow! (4th Grade Edition)

Client Handout: 3 Type of Play	What Your Brain Is Doing	Why It Is Good for You	Examples	What Do You Like?
Running Around	Your brain and body are working together	Helps you stay healthy and feel happy	Tag, jumping, riding bikes	🏃♂
Making Jokes	Your brain is being silly and smart	Helps you laugh and make friends	Telling jokes, funny faces	😄
Making Things	Your brain is being creative	Helps you solve problems and feel proud	Drawing, LEGO, crafts	🎨
Playing Games	Your brain follows rules and makes choices	Helps you learn teamwork and fairness	Board games, card games	🎲
Acting or Pretending	Your brain is imagining and remembering	Helps you learn stories and express feelings	Dress-up, animal play	🎭
Thinking Big Ideas	Your brain is wondering and dreaming	Helps you ask questions and grow your thoughts	Daydreaming, "what if" games	💭

Counseling Goals for PLAY (Neurobiological Perspective)

Goal: To help the client access, express, and sustain safe, reciprocal social engagement by reactivating the PLAY system through embodied experiences, while supporting the integration of emotional regulation, spontaneity, and relational joy.

Rationale: The PLAY system is a deeply ingrained social-emotional circuit that promotes flexible thinking, resilience, and learning through joyful, reciprocal engagement. Neurochemically, PLAY is associated with the release of endogenous opioids, dopamine, and oxytocin: neurotransmitters that reinforce safety, bonding, and exploratory behavior. Neuroanatomically, PLAY involves subcortical regions such as the dorsomedial thalamus, PAG, and areas of the basal ganglia, which coordinate rhythmic movements and affective synchrony (Panksepp & Biven, 2012). When children (or adults) are play-deprived, whether due to trauma, chronic stress, or neurodevelopmental differences, the neural circuits for spontaneity, laughter, and co-regulation often go offline or become inhibited by fear and vigilance systems.

Clinical Application: Therapeutically, the goal is to re-engage the PLAY system by introducing moments of lightness, curiosity, and movement into the therapeutic process. This may involve rhythm-based activities, shared creative tasks, nonverbal mirroring, or metaphorical storytelling. The aim is to gently lower defensive arousal and reawaken the capacity for safe exploration and mutual joy.

This is especially important in clients who have had limited opportunities for joyful expression, whether due to early adversity, neglect, or rigid environmental expectations. In these cases, PLAY becomes not just an emotional system, but a route back to vitality, connection, and social learning. Ultimately, the work supports the reintegration of bottom-up feelings of safety and spontaneity with top-down capacities for engagement and reflection.

Therapeutic Touchpoints/Goals for PLAY in the Affective Inventory Framework

The ideas the client should walk away with:

1 PLAY Is a Core Emotional System That Builds Social Intelligence, Creativity, and Joy
PLAY is not just recreational, it is essential for brain development, emotional resilience, and relationship-building. In Panksepp's model, PLAY is a biologically hardwired system that supports learning, emotional regulation, and the development of empathy through joyful interaction. This system teaches boundaries, cooperation, and emotional give-and-take long before language is fully developed.

2 The PLAY System Builds the Brain from the Bottom Up
PLAY strengthens neural connections between motor, emotional, and cognitive systems. Rough-and-tumble play, pretend games, and shared laughter all stimulate critical regions like the prefrontal cortex, cerebellum, and basal ganglia. These activities enhance executive functioning, impulse control, and emotional regulation in children and adults alike.

3 PLAY Is a Practice Ground for Safe Social Risk
Through PLAY, individuals learn how to test boundaries, experience failure without shame, and repair ruptures in real time. It helps the nervous system tolerate surprise, adapt to rules, and explore power dynamics safely. For trauma-affected individuals, PLAY offers a reparative experience of spontaneity, safety, and control that may have been absent in early life.

4 Laughter, Pretend, and Imagination Are Forms of Emotional Rehearsal
PLAY allows children (and adults) to simulate real-world emotions in manageable doses. Pretending to be scared, angry, or sad within the safety of a game helps integrate affective experiences. This builds emotional fluency and improves one's capacity to express and tolerate strong feelings in daily life.
5 PLAY Is a State of Nervous System Safety
The PLAY system functions optimally when the ventral vagal complex (the "social engagement" branch of the parasympathetic nervous system) is active (Porges, 2011). This means PLAY is only possible when the brain is not in a threat state. If a child or adult cannot play, it is often a sign that the nervous system does not feel safe enough yet.
6 Trauma, Stress, and Shame Can Suppress the PLAY System, but It Can Be Reactivated
Children who have experienced trauma may appear rigid, overly serious, or shut down during situations where play would normally emerge. Adults who were raised in high-stress, punitive, or emotionally barren environments may struggle with spontaneity and joy. Re-engaging in PLAY, especially in safe, attuned relationships, can help restore curiosity and affective vitality.
7 PLAY Builds Attachment Through Joyful Shared Experience
Joy is the glue of early attachment, and PLAY is its delivery system. Mutual eye contact, shared laughter, physical games, and rhythmic interactions are how caregiver and child synchronize emotionally. These moments release oxytocin, dopamine, and endogenous opioids, building trust and relational safety. In therapy, PLAY can repair attachment wounds by recreating these micro-moments of attunement.
8 PLAY Is Not Frivolous; It Is Foundational
Too often, PLAY is undervalued in favor of academic performance, obedience, or "maturity". But playfulness supports flexible thinking, emotional adaptability, and resilience. Clients should be encouraged to rediscover PLAY not just as a childhood phase, but as an essential adult need for pleasure, creativity, and meaningful connection.
9 PLAY Can Be Reintroduced Gently and Intentionally
For clients who struggle with PLAY, therapeutic work may include expressive arts, improvisational storytelling, cooperative games, or playful social interactions. The goal is not to perform but to experience unstructured, reciprocal joy. These experiences help restore a sense of agency and reduce defensiveness.
10 Healing Through PLAY Is Not Just Possible: It is Powerful
PLAY reawakens parts of the self that have been silenced by stress, shame, or grief. It allows clients to explore new identities, express feelings safely, and engage the world with renewed openness. When PLAY is integrated with other core emotional systems, it acts as a bridge between safety, creativity, and deep social connection.

Client Handout 4: The PLAY System: Your Brain's Natural Way of Learning Through Fun and Connection

Client Handout 4: The PLAY System	Description
What Is PLAY?	PLAY is your brain's "have fun" system. It makes you want to giggle, pretend, move around, and enjoy being with others in a joyful way
How Can I Tell It Is On?	You feel silly, light, happy, or bouncy. You might laugh, joke, or run around. You enjoy sharing time and ideas with other people
Why Is It So Important?	PLAY helps you connect with others and learn new things without pressure. It builds trust, flexibility, creativity, and resilience
What Turns It Off?	Feeling embarrassed, judged, unsafe, or pressured can shut it down. Stress, sadness, or fear can also make it hard to feel playful
How Do We Turn It Back On?	Make space for laughter and silliness. Try games, roleplay, or anything that helps you feel free to be yourself. It helps to be around people who make you feel safe and happy
Is Imagination Part of PLAY?	Yes! Pretending, storytelling, and goofing around are key parts of PLAY. They help your brain grow while you're having fun
What Helps It Work Best?	Being with others who are kind and open to having fun. Environments that feel safe and relaxed. Time for unstructured, spontaneous play
Can It Get Tricked?	Sometimes we confuse screen time or overstimulation for PLAY, but true PLAY involves imagination, interaction, and movement
What If I've Lost It?	You can find it again. Start with small, playful moments like humor, games, drawing, or a funny face. PLAY lives inside you all the time, it just needs the right space to come out
Why Does It Matter in Counseling?	PLAY helps your brain heal, connect, and grow. It is how kids build emotional skills and how adults rediscover joy. PLAY makes therapy more effective and more pleasant

In addition, here are some ideas for questions that can help the client incorporate the ideas about the emotion into their everyday life:

Client Reflection Handout: My PLAY System

1 What kind of play makes you laugh or feel happy?

2 When do you feel the most free and silly?

3 Who do you enjoy playing with the most, and why?

4 What helps you feel safe enough to be playful?

5 What's one playful thing you'd like to do more often?

Draw Your PLAY Self!
Use the space below to draw what your PLAY system looks like when it is working. You can draw yourself playing, laughing, pretending, or doing something fun with others.

Note: A downloadable version of this handout is available via the webpage for the book at: www.routledge.com/9781041250135

References

Gray, P. (2013). *Free to learn: Why unleashing the instinct to play will make our children happier, more self-reliant, and better students for life*. Basic Books.

Kolb, B., & Whishaw, I. (2020). *Fundamentals of human neuroscience* (8th ed.). Worth.

Panksepp, J. (1998a). *Affective neuroscience: The foundations of human and animal emotions*. Oxford University Press.

Panksepp, J. (1998b). The periconscious substrates of consciousness: Affective states and the evolutionary origins of the SELF. *Journal of Consciousness Studies*, 5(5–6), 566–582

Panksepp, J. (2003). At the interface between the affective, behavioral, and cognitive neurosciences: Decoding the emotional feelings of the brain. *Brain and Cognition*, 52(1), 4–14.

Panksepp, J. (2005a). Affective consciousness: Core emotional feelings in animals and humans. *Consciousness and Cognition*, 14(1), 30–80.

Panksepp, J. (2005b). On the embodied neural nature of the core emotional affects. *Journal of Consciousness Studies*, 12(8–10), 158–184.

Panksepp, J. (2006a). Emotional endophenotypes in evolutionary psychiatry. *Progress in Neuro-Psychopharmacology & Biological Psychiatry*, 30(5), 774–784.

Panksepp, J. (2006b). The core emotional systems of the mammalian brain: The fundamental substrates of human emotions. In H. Corrigall, H. Payne, & I. Wilkinson (Eds.), *About a body: Working with the embodied mind in psychotherapy* (pp. 14–32). Routledge.

Panksepp, J., & Biven, L. (2012). *The archaeology of mind: Neuroevolutionary origins of human emotions*. W. W. Norton.

Pellis, S. M., & Pellis, V. C. (2009). *The playful brain: Venturing to the limits of neuroscience*. Oneworld Publications.

Porges, S. W. (2011). *The polyvagal theory: Neurophysiological foundations of emotions, attachment, communication, and self-regulation*. W. W. Norton & Company.

Chapter 9

SAD (PANIC/GRIEF)

Note: The label of PANIC/GRIEF will be represented with the common term of SAD. This is a more generic term that might better traverse the continuum of PANIC/GRIEF and is probably more child friendly. However, the clinician should use the term that is best suited to the client. All three terms are acceptable.

Allostatic Purpose of SAD

While ANGER is about exerting energy to create or protect a boundary, and PLAY is about feeding growth through exciting exploration, SAD is quite the opposite in its energy level and purpose. SAD is about sitting with the loss of how things could or should be. We humans are always looking for opportunity and resources but when something happens that takes our thriving away, we have to accept it so we can adjust to a new set of parameters. It requires that we evaluate the level of loss, find a way to integrate it into our immediate and life plans and reorganize how we are going to go forward. It does not feel good. Loss of any kind is painful (literally). Sometimes the loss is temporary, and we recalibrate quickly and sometimes it is devastating, and we lose our hold on our sense-of-self and the world around us. Of course, we can also have lots of little losses that pile up and cumulatively require extensive recalibration such as working for a toxic boss and reaching a point when we are miserable going to work every day. We can also have a large loss that is remediated quickly such as losing a job and finding another immediately. Some losses we see coming and many we do not. This is why allostasis (predicting the environment) is such an important construct for the understanding of the SAD core emotion. It has a purpose that directly impacts survival.

Allostasis is not just about maintaining biological system parameters in the body; that is under the purview of homeostasis. Allostasis is about feedforward and feedback functioning. The mind-brain has to constantly predict what things are going on in the environment that are positive and negative and adjust in real-time to minimize prediction errors and loss. When we experience loss, we have to recalibrate, so we do not experience more loss and re-evaluate how we are to go on with the loss. It is the price that humans have to pay because we are vulnerable mammals that only have our brains to outmaneuver threats in the environment. When things go wrong and we experience loss we feel pain and we don't like it. We know at some level we have to spend some

DOI: 10.4324/9781003745686-11

time figuring out how our safe world became a painful one so we can fix it and prevent it from happening again. Therefore, SAD feelings are a direct message from the self saying, "that is not good for you or within your control to change so figure out how you are going to go forward".

Why is SAD so painful? It is because at some level we know what has happened might be tolerable, but it is not helpful to our survival. In fact, we know at some level, that SAD is undermining our ability to thrive. Painful core emotions are wonderful alert systems that force us to understand what is going on so we can act and return to a reasonable state of allostasis. In the case of SAD, that action is to go deep inside and rethink about our values, support systems, likes, dislikes, moral values and find something to replace the loss. We certainly would not do this deep revamping if it was pleasant. Pleasant means we are doing ok and feel safe; unpleasant means work toward changing something because this is not going to go away until you do *and* over time it will erode your ability to use other emotions that help you through this period. Pain is therefore the impetus for readjustment.

For the most part, we experience every day small losses and can get away with putting off recalibration until we have time to process it out. When losses do not get processed over time or the losses are greater in nature, then sorting things out requires that we go deep because we may have to make deep changes to our lives. When we go deep, we see a decrease in our SEEKING, PLAY, and other core positive emotions and, in essence, are not using all our emotion skills to thrive. This powering down of positive core emotions therefore leaves us vulnerable; we are not on our game and in the world of survival we are less dynamic and flexible. So, on the one hand we need to power down and take time to route around our core self and on the other hand, we need to protect ourselves while we are not at our best. Hence, folks dealing with loss tend to protect themselves by isolating, pulling back from engaging in life events, sleeping a lot, eating too much or too little, and showing dull affect. They have work to do and it takes a lot of internal energy to do it.

From this perspective, we can see why SAD is accompanied by FEAR and ANGER a lot. Individuals who have not figured out the recalibration may be anxious if they cannot see a way out and may be worried about being vulnerable or worried about the prospect that things will never change. Here lies the helpless and hopeless model of depression where individuals feel that they cannot change the pain or make it work for them. The future looks bleak as they envision always feeling this way. There is a perception of an external locus of control from the environment and a life where they have no agency. We humans love our agency! It brings us balance and sustains us when things are tough with the promise or hope that we can make things better. Individuals who are doing their SAD work may also have angry bursts because recalibration can be a long and uncomfortable process or perhaps the world needs a boundary, so people leave them alone to do their work.

Physiology and Neuroanatomical Features of SAD

Perhaps one of the most interesting developments in neuroscientific research about pain is A. Bud Craig's (Craig, 2009; Craig, 2010) position that the pain of sadness is rooted in the interplay between interoception, the insular cortex, and homeostatic drives and emotions. As mentioned in the Introduction to this book, Craig's work showed that physical and emotional pain share the same neural pathways into the brain. It was thought in the past that these interoceptive signals from the body went only to the sensory cortex, and many times they do (for physical pain injuries etc.). However, the major revelation in his work is that the homeostatic feelings in the body that include physical and emotional pain report to the anterior insula which is the main hub for the translation of bodily feelings to the frontal cortex where decisions are made. There is an interplay in the insula of survival messages from the body with the individual's ability to sense internal changes and adjust behaviors accordingly.

Craig's work spearheaded a growing body of research that suggests that social pain (such as being excluded from a group and social isolation) and physical pain overlap in the pathways from the body up to the insular cortex. They also share biological regulatory systems such as oxytocin (the love cuddle neurohormone) and endogenous opioids. Craig also proposed, that from an evolutionary perspective, a shared neural system for processing both physical and emotional pain was adaptive for our ancestors. Social connection was critical for survival in early human communities and pain would spur avoidance of separation.

Jaak Panksepp also strongly believed that social loss and physical pain are deeply entwined because of shared neurochemistry and brain systems (Panksepp, 1998a; 1998b; 2003; 2005a; 2005b; 2006a; 2006b; Panksepp & Biven, 2012) as his work focused on SAD as originating from separation distress in mammals. His studies show that across species, separation of babies from caregivers gives rise to highly specific distress calls. Their calls are loud, and from a practical point of view the acoustics register not only the level of the infant's distress and panic (because at some deep level the child knows they will not survive if left alone) but registers rapid alerts in adults around the infant. This distressed state was coined as PANIC/GRIEF system by Panksepp as he observed separated offspring increase distress calls, show dysregulated body systems, and resolution into grief and despair. These observations allowed Panksepp to discover and map the specific pathways for SAD and create the basis for understanding the origin of the continuum of the SAD emotion. In other words, mammals need to develop strong bonds in a social manner for survival and the loss of the bond is critical and painful. When bonding and attachment are secure, the neurochemicals are pleasurable and sustained. When bonds are broken, uncomfortable stress hormones take over. This is how nature cements the social bonds that humans need to survive. In essence, feeling good in our lives is dependent on breathing the social air around us at all times. When we are around our support family, group, team, or class we know, at some deep level, that we have a better chance of surviving. Of course, the contrary is true as well; when our social system is problematic or toxic then we are left in an isolated state to defend ourselves. It is easy to picture this in primitive man as the social bond and life in general was so physically close to just being about survival. But what about today's world? When we have enough food, shelter, and assets to be able to not be dependent on anyone for anything? Do we still hark back to distress calls and panic if separated in this way? Does it set us up for depression if we live this way? The answer is, yes. Research mapping this separation-distress system has identified circuitry extending from the dorsal periaqueductal gray (PAG) to the anterior cingulate cortex, activated by glutamate and corticotropin-releasing factor (CRF), and inhibited by endogenous opioids, oxytocin, and prolactin: essential neurochemicals for social attachment and bonding.

Panksepp suggested that depression could arise from a dysfunction in the interplay between the SEEKING and PANIC/GRIEF systems. Specifically, he proposed that diminished activity of the SEEKING system, which motivates goal-directed behavior, alongside the persistence of the psychological pain associated with the SAD system, could contribute to the development of depressive states. Panksepp also found declining opioid, oxytocin, and prolactin levels coupled with increased stress hormones with this system. Panksepp's findings suggested to him that the pain of depression, arising mostly from social loss and isolation may be the price that humans pay for the evolutionary advantages of social bonds that enrich our lives and promote survival.

Cultural Factors

It is important to remember that SAD, like all emotions, is culture bound and may be expressed differently depending on the individual's socioeconomic status, sex, gender, racial, ethnic, ableness, and other cultural factors. The SAD system is shaped not only by neurobiology but also by cultural context. While the capacity to experience grief and longing is universal, the expression, suppression, and resolution of SAD are deeply influenced by cultural beliefs, norms, and relational practices.

In collectivist cultures, for example, emotional expressions of SAD may be ritualized and community-based, allowing for shared mourning, vocal grieving, and public displays of loss. In contrast, individualistic cultures may privatize or suppress emotional expression, reinforcing a "grieve quietly and move on" narrative that can leave individuals feeling isolated in their pain (Klass et al., 1996).

Cultural attitudes toward death, attachment, and emotional vulnerability shape how people interpret the SAD response. Some cultures provide structured mourning periods, symbolic rituals, and multi-generational support that serve to co-regulate the nervous system and allow for the safe completion of the grief process (Porges, 2011). Others may minimize or pathologize sadness, especially in men or marginalized groups, resulting in inhibited SAD expression that later manifests as somatic symptoms, irritability, or emotional disconnection.

Historical trauma, displacement, colonization, and racism can also amplify and complicate SAD responses. For many individuals who have been marginalized, the SAD system is chronically activated by repeated relational and systemic losses such as the loss of cultural identity, safety, or intergenerational belonging. These lived realities may not always be seen as "grief" in a Western clinical model, but they can represent persistent disruptions in attachment and safety.

Finally, spiritual and religious frameworks also shape grief regulation. Some belief systems offer afterlife narratives that reframe death as continuity, soothing the biological pain of separation. Others emphasize restraint or divine will, encouraging containment over expression. The degree to which these frameworks support emotional integration varies by individual experience and social support.

Continuum of Expression of SAD

Table 9.1 outlines the progression of SAD across five distinct levels from mainstream typical, healthy experiences of sadness to more severe and clinically significant forms. Each level is accompanied by key neurobiological patterns and the functional role that sadness may serve at that stage. The continuum illustrates how sadness, while often uncomfortable, can have adaptive value until it becomes dysregulated and impairs functioning. This framework supports clinicians in identifying where a client's emotional state may fall along the spectrum and guides intervention by connecting emotional experiences to neural circuitry and purpose.

Practical Translation SAD

In general, the best way to help our students with the SAD core emotion is to first help them identify when they are sad and then help them switch to thinking about what SAD is trying to tell them. It has a message that something has to change in their lives. Something must be readjusted so they can cope and return to balance.

Time is of the essence when it comes to intervening with SAD. So, we know that SAD is loss and if we do not fix it then it can descend into reduced functioning of positive brain systems (and their healthy chemistry) over time. The longer it goes on the less physically capable we are of doing the actual work that will help us recalibrate. We descend into a helpless and hopeless state that requires a neurochemical jump start (possibly medications), a loving support system, an accomplished counselor, and the patience for a slow ascendency back to agency. Of course, this supposes that the individual at some point in their upbringing has experienced agency so they can come back to it. But what about those children who experienced very early SAD? Edward

Table 9.1 Continuum of SAD Expression

Level	Description	Neural Correlates	Functional Role
1. Normative Sadness	Brief, context-appropriate emotional response (e.g. grief after a loss or disappointment)	Moderate activation of subgenual anterior cingulate cortex (sgACC), amygdala, and insula	Supports emotional learning, enhances social bonding, encourages reflection and empathy
2. Prolonged Sadness	Sadness persists beyond expected duration; marked by rumination but not significantly impairing	Increased activity in the default mode network (DMN); mild dysregulation in prefrontal-limbic circuits	Promotes re-evaluation of goals and priorities; can foster resilience and adaptation
3. Subclinical Depression	Pervasive low mood with mild impairment (e.g. reduced motivation, interest); not meeting criteria for MDD	Hypoactivity in dorsolateral prefrontal cortex (dlPFC); hyperactivity in the amygdala; decreased serotonergic tone	May conserve energy and signal need for environmental or interpersonal change
4. Major Depressive Episode	Persistent sadness with cognitive, somatic, and emotional symptoms; significant daily impairment	Hypoactivity in reward networks (ventral striatum, vmPFC); hyperconnectivity in DMN; serotonin, dopamine, and norepinephrine imbalances	Disrupts adaptive emotion regulation; reflects breakdown in internal self-regulatory systems

Level	Description	Neural Correlates	Functional Role
5. Pathological/ Refractory Sadness	Chronic or treatment-resistant depression, including melancholic or psychotic features; possible suicidal ideation	Structural atrophy in hippocampus, anterior cingulate cortex (ACC), and prefrontal cortex; overactive HPA axis; neuro-inflammation	Emotion becomes non-functional; severely impairs cognition, safety, and overall well-being

Tronick's (2007) work on attachment is a must read for those of us who work with children and youth with trauma and depression. Without treatment, the dysregulation experienced in infancy becomes the baseline for a personality profile that leads to very poor life outcomes as illustrated by the large body of research on the ACE's questionnaire (Felitti, 1998).

Understanding the functional purpose of SAD helps us understand how to intervene. Those children and youth who are affected by persistent sadness need us to help them regain balance so that their SEEKING, PLAY, and CARE systems come back online. The latter, in a sense, are the keys to resilience and it is very difficult to bounce back from SAD events if the individual is low in these systems. For the youth with sadness, it is difficult for them to think of activities that bring them joy. They usually subscribe positive events to something outside coming to them as opposed to them intentionally creating opportunities for agency. This external versus internal locus of control perception leaves agency to random things happening in their environment. They know that external happiness, for them, is fleeting and they mourn the loss of the happy feeling before it is even gone.

As counselors and advocates we have to first help the child understand the meaning of SAD and then guide them through how to change their locus of control to be internally mediated. This means that we have to let them know about the arsenal of emotions that they have at their disposal to handle anything that life throws at them. They must be in touch with what each core emotion feels like in their bodies, they must accept that these emotions are real in all humans, they must be able to understand that their families may or may not have modeled these emotions for them, and they must understand the practical value of each emotion as a tool for living given to them by biology and evolution. This process is a heavy lifting job for the counselor but youth who are SAD are attracted like moths to a flame when their counselor shows certainty that positive emotions are in all of us that and can be tapped at any time.

Grief

We need to say a few words about the worst of sad feelings, grief. Panksepp has described it as the motherload of SAD and he spent quite a bit of time exploring this core emotion in depth (Panksepp, 1998a; 1998b; 2003; 2005a; 2005b; 2006a; 2006b; Panksepp & Biven, 2012).

He suggested that while the neuroanatomical and neurochemical changes in the brain and body are very similar with SAD and grief, the latter changes usually unfold across time. When we experience the major event of death of a loved one, our brains initiate a complex neurochemical and neuroanatomical reaction that reflects both the pain of separation and the longing for connection. As with all SAD feelings, grief activates the same brain regions involved in physical pain, reward processing, emotional regulation, and memory (Craig, 2009).

In the earliest stages of grief, the amygdala, a region involved in fear and emotional salience, becomes highly reactive. It works closely with the insula, which helps us interpret internal emotional states, and the subgenual anterior cingulate cortex (sgACC), which modulates sadness and integrates emotional pain. These regions are central to the experience of acute grief, especially when we encounter reminders of the person we have lost.

Grief is also a story of disrupted attachment. The nucleus accumbens, a structure typically associated with pleasure and reward, plays an unexpected role. In cases of prolonged or complicated grief, this region remains persistently activated, almost as if the brain is "craving" the lost connection. This response mirrors the neural pattern seen in addiction and suggests that unresolved grief might function like a persistent longing rather than a fading sorrow. At the same time, the medial prefrontal cortex responsible for social cognition, empathy, and autobiographical memory struggles to integrate the absence of the loved one into a coherent narrative. This contributes to the disorientation and cognitive fog often reported in grief and especially difficult for children and youth.

The hippocampus, known for memory formation and emotional context, can shrink over time if chronic stress persists. Elevated levels of cortisol, the primary stress hormone, are common in grief, especially when it becomes prolonged. Sustained cortisol exposure not only disrupts mood and sleep but can lead to neurotoxicity in sensitive brain areas like the hippocampus compounding emotional and possibly behavioral dysregulation.

Neurochemically, grief alters the delicate balance of mood-regulating systems. Serotonin levels often decline, contributing to sadness, insomnia, and appetite changes. Dopamine (the primary neurochemical associated with SEEKING) which motivates us toward goals and pleasures, may also decrease, intensifying feelings of emptiness and fatigue. Meanwhile, oxytocin, the "bonding hormone", may become dysregulated, weakening the protective buffer of social connection and making loneliness feel more acute.

Interestingly, our bodies' natural pain relievers, endogenous opioids, also decline during grief. This may explain the physical pain often associated with deep emotional loss. The result is a multi-system experience: psychological pain, physical discomfort, and profound neurochemical shifts that can either resolve over time or spiral into pathology.

As grief progresses, the brain's core emotions typically work toward recalibration. Regions in the default mode network, responsible for self-reflection and mental time travel, begin to re-engage in healthy ways. When mourning is adaptive, these networks help us make meaning out of loss, integrate the experience into the child's life narrative, and eventually restore emotional equilibrium.

However, when grief becomes complicated or prolonged, or if the loss occurs at an early age where higher levels of cognition are immature, these same systems may remain in a kind of neurological limbo. The longing doesn't fade, and the neural architecture of sadness becomes entrenched. Grief, in essence, is a reflection of connection. It is the price of love. Its pain is evidence of our capacity to bond deeply and its resolution, when it comes, is a testament to the brain's remarkable ability to reorganize, adapt, and eventually find peace (Panksepp & Biven, 2012).

Interesting Note About Tears

Tears are far more than a sign of sadness or frustration and they are a complex psychobiological process with functions that span physiology, emotion regulation, and social communication.

Research now shows that tears serve adaptive roles not only for the individual shedding them, but for those witnessing them (Hendriks et al., 2008).

There are three types of tears: basal, reflex, and emotional (or psychic), the latter of which are uniquely human. They emerge in moments of deep affect: grief, joy, relief, awe, or overwhelming connection. Unlike reflex tears, which protect the eyes from irritants, emotional tears appear to serve neuropsychological and interpersonal purposes.

Neurochemically, emotional tears contain stress-related biochemicals such as cortisol, adrenocorticotropic hormone, prolactin, and leucine enkephalin, a natural painkiller. This supports the idea that crying may help detoxify stress, down-regulate arousal, and restore homeostasis in the autonomic nervous system. It is a kind of natural reset button for overwhelming emotional states (Vingerhoets, 2013; Vingerhoets & Bylsma, 2016).

From a neuroscience perspective, crying involves the anterior cingulate cortex, insula, hypothalamus, and brainstem nuclei, regions associated with social pain, attachment, and autonomic regulation. Emotional crying often co-occurs with parasympathetic rebound with slower heart rate, deep exhalations, and a feeling of release (Newman, 2007).

For children, tears may elicit caregiving responses, which may be evolutionarily designed to keep them close to protection when they are dysregulated or in distress. In adults, visible tears can evoke empathy, reduce conflict, or signal authenticity (Panksepp & Biven, 2012).

Early cultural experiences shape how a child learns to self-regulate, express needs, and relate to vulnerability. Gender differences also emerge early as girls are often allowed to cry more freely, while boys may learn to suppress tears, potentially at a cost to emotional processing. Crying is obviously not a weakness from a biological point of view but is a neurodevelopmentally intelligent behavior. It is a signal that the child's nervous system has reached a threshold and is seeking regulation. When met with attuned, regulated caregiving, the act of crying can strengthen attachment, promote emotional literacy, and facilitate healing.

Practical Translation of Grief

In terms of school interventions, my main concern is how do we allow youth to fully grieve in a school that has daily demands that require being fully present and emotionally balanced? Major grief destroys emotional balance for some time and yet we many times expect children to bounce back immediately. So many times, I have seen educational personnel expect children who have lost a close family member to meet educational tasks in a few weeks. I understand that we do not want the child to lose important information and not be able to maintain their grades, but this concern can easily turn into another stressor for the child at a time when they don't need further stress. From a brain perspective, it might actually be impossible. It is also a situation that is heavily guided by cultural practices and sometimes these are at odds with school expectations.

Counseling Goals for SAD (Neurobiological Perspective)

Goal: To help the client identify, tolerate, and process feelings of separation, loss, and loneliness by reestablishing emotional safety, supporting social reconnection, and promoting healing within the SAD system.

Rationale: The SAD system, often experienced subjectively as deep sadness, despair, or longing, is a core emotional network designed to protest social separation and elicit care and reconnection. Neurochemically, this system is regulated by endogenous opioids, oxytocin, and CRF. During activation such as in grief, abandonment, or emotional loss opioid levels drop and CRF rises, leading to the acute emotional pain of separation distress.

Neuroanatomically, SAD involves the anterior cingulate cortex (ACC), periaqueductal gray (PAG), dorsomedial thalamus, and connections to the amygdala and hypothalamus. These structures are involved in vocal crying, social signaling, autonomic distress, and attachment repair. When chronically activated without resolution, this system may contribute to depression, emotional withdrawal, or excessive dependency.

Clinical Application: Therapeutically, the goal is to create a safe and responsive relational space where the client can grieve, name their losses, and begin to tolerate the intensity of separation-related affect. This may involve gently helping the client connect their interoceptive sensations (e.g. heaviness in the chest, lump in the throat) to specific emotional states and life events.

In clients with attachment trauma, ambiguous loss, or unresolved grief, the SAD system may be over- or under-activated. It can present as either emotional flooding and clinging, or emotional shutdown and avoidance. Supporting this system involves validating emotional pain, helping the client articulate what they needed but did not receive, and guiding them to mourn what was lost while also discovering new pathways to connection.

Ultimately, counseling with this system in mind emphasizes that sadness is not a symptom to eliminate, but a biologically meaningful emotional state that calls for contact, comfort, and integration. Healing occurs not by denying the pain of disconnection, but by making space for it so the client can metabolize their grief, reconnect to self and others, and feel accompanied in their experience.

Therapeutic Touchpoints/Goals for SAD in the Affective Inventory Framework

The ideas the client should walk away with:

1 SAD Is the Brain's Separation Distress System; It Signals Loss, Not Defect
This system is evolutionarily designed to protest separation from attachment figures. Crying, longing, and social pain are not signs of weakness; they are biologically wired survival responses that motivate reconnection. When clients feel overwhelming sadness after rejection or loss, it means their emotional system is working as nature intended.

2 We Are Born Expecting Connection: SAD Activates When It Is Lost
Infants cannot survive alone, so the brain developed a system to sound the alarm when separation occurs. This system that centered in the dorsal anterior cingulate cortex, periaqueductal gray, and dorsomedial thalamus produces the unbearable ache of abandonment. For children, this may look like inconsolable crying; for adults, it may feel like heartbreak, despair, or numbness.

3 Separation Distress Can Leave a Lasting Imprint on the Nervous System
When early caregiving is inconsistent or ruptured by trauma, neglect, or abandonment, the SAD system may become hypersensitive. This shows up later as attachment anxiety, fear of rejection, or intense emotional reactions to even minor relational slights. Understanding these as grief responses (not overreactions) helps reduce shame and increase self-compassion.

4 Grief Is Not Just About Death: It Is About the Loss of Safety, Connection, or Hope
Clients often grieve the parent they never had, the love they didn't receive, or the version of themselves that got lost in chaos. Therapy should normalize non-death losses and help clients put words to ambiguous grief, disenfranchised grief, and early emotional losses that still echo in their adult lives.

5 Crying, Longing, and Protest Are Expressions of the SAD System
These responses are not signs of emotional instability they are the brain's way of trying to reconnect. When children cry out after a parent leaves, or when adults feel sudden anguish after abandonment, it is the SAD system doing its job. These behaviors are relational communication not dysfunction.

6 If SAD Is Chronic or Unattended; It Can Lead to Numbing or Withdrawal
When the system is activated repeatedly without comfort or resolution, the brain may shut it down to protect itself. This can result in flattened affect, detachment, or even alexithymia (difficulty identifying feelings). Therapy helps to "reawaken" this system gently, so that grief can move again rather than remain stuck.

7 Healing the SAD System Requires Connection and Witnessing
The antidote to separation distress is not distraction or toughness. It is safe reconnection. Whether through a therapist, a friend, a caregiver, or even a pet, the client must experience what it means to be held in grief without being fixed, abandoned, or judged. Grief needs a witness to metabolize.

8 SAD Is Tied to Our Capacity for Love, Empathy, and Meaning
The same system that breaks our heart when someone leaves also gives our relationships depth and meaning. Grief is the cost of caring. Helping clients understand this paradox can transform their pain into something honorable: a reflection of how deeply they feel, not how broken they are.

9 Grief Has a Rhythm But It Does Not Follow a Straight Line
Clients should be reminded that grief does not obey schedules. It surges, recedes, loops, and evolves. Progress is not about feeling better fast, but about allowing space for the full range of emotions: sadness, anger, relief, confusion, and hope. Therapy offers structure for that unfolding process.

10 The SAD System Is Also a Gateway to Growth and Reconnection
When held safely, grief can become a portal to deeper self-awareness, compassion, and emotional resilience. The goal is not to suppress grief but to understand it, hold it with care, and use it to reorient the self toward meaning, connection, and future relationships.

Client Handout 5: The SAD System: Your Brain's Way of Asking for Connection and Comfort

Client Handout 5: SAD	Description
What Is SAD?	It is your brain's connection system. It turns on when you feel separation, loss, or deep sadness. It makes you want comfort, closeness, and care
How Can I Tell It Is On?	You might cry, feel empty or lonely, want a hug, or feel like hiding. Your chest may ache, or your body may feel heavy or tired
Why Is It So Important?	This system helps you connect to others. It shows that you care and want closeness. When sadness is supported, it helps you heal and feel loved again
What Turns It Off?	Comfort, connection, and feeling safe can calm this system. Being listened to and hugged helps sadness settle down
How Can We Take Care of It?	Let yourself feel the sadness. Talk to someone you trust. Write, draw, or cry, It is okay to feel. Comforting yourself gently is healing
Is It Okay to Feel Sad a Lot?	Sometimes, yes. But if sadness feels too big or doesn't go away, It is a sign you might need more support. You're not alone, help is out there
What Helps It Work Best?	Safe people, quiet spaces, and comforting routines help this system feel calm. Pets, blankets, or kind words can be very soothing too
Can It Get Stuck?	Yes. If sadness stays too long, it can lead to deep loneliness or hopelessness. That's not your fault, it means your brain needs help reconnecting
What If Someone Doesn't Understand?	That's hard. But your feelings are real, and someone out there will listen. It is okay to keep looking for the right listener or helper
Why Does It Matter in Counseling?	Sadness shows us what we need. Therapy helps us feel seen, supported, and able to reconnect after loss. It reminds us that we're not alone

In addition, here are some ideas for questions that can help the client incorporate the ideas about the emotion into their everyday life:

Client Reflection Handout: My SAD System

1. What helps you feel better when you're sad or missing someone?

2. Who do you trust to talk to or hug when you feel alone?

3. What's something comforting you can do when you're sad (like music, drawing, or a walk)?

4. What do you wish people knew about your sadness?

5. What's one small step that helps you feel less alone?

Draw Your Comforting Connection!
Use the space below to draw what helps you feel safe and loved. It could be a favorite person, place, animal, or something that brings comfort when you feel sad.

Note: A downloadable version of this handout is available via the webpage for the book at: www.routledge.com/9781041250135

References

Craig, A. D. (2009). How do you feel—now? The anterior insula and human awareness. *Nature Reviews Neuroscience*, 10(1), 59–70. https://doi.org/10.1038/nrn2555

Craig, A. D. (2010). The sentient self. *Brain Structure and Function*, 214(5–6), 563–577. https://doi.org/10.1007/s00429-010-0248-y

Felitti, V. J., Anda, R. F., Nordenberg, D., Williamson, D. F., Spitz, A. M., Edwards, V., Koss, M. P., & Marks, J. S. (1998). Relationship of childhood abuse and household dysfunction to many of the leading causes of death in adults. *American Journal of Preventive Medicine*, 14(4), 245–258.

Hendriks, M. C. P., Croon, M. A., & Vingerhoets, A. J. J. M. (2008). Social reactions to adult crying: The help-soliciting function of tears. *Journal of Nonverbal Behavior*, 32, 95–118.

Klass, D., Silverman, P. R., & Nickman, S. (1996). *Continuing bonds: New understandings of grief*. Taylor & Francis.

Newman, J. D. (2007). Neural circuits underlying crying and laughter in animals and humans. In J. Panksepp (Ed.), *Textbook of biological psychiatry* (pp. 313–328). Wiley.

Panksepp, J. (1998a). *Affective neuroscience: The foundations of human and animal emotions*. Oxford University Press.

Panksepp, J. (1998b). The periconscious substrates of consciousness: Affective states and the evolutionary origins of the SELF. *Journal of Consciousness Studies*, 5(5–6), 566–582.

Panksepp, J. (2003). At the interface between the affective, behavioral, and cognitive neurosciences: Decoding the emotional feelings of the brain. *Brain and Cognition*, 52(1), 4–14.

Panksepp, J. (2005a). Affective consciousness: Core emotional feelings in animals and humans. *Consciousness and Cognition*, 14(1), 30–80.

Panksepp, J. (2005b). On the embodied neural nature of the core emotional affects. *Journal of Consciousness Studies*, 12(8–10), 158–184.

Panksepp, J. (2006a). Emotional endophenotypes in evolutionary psychiatry. *Progress in Neuro-Psychopharmacology & Biological Psychiatry*, 30(5), 774–784.

Panksepp, J. (2006b). The core emotional systems of the mammalian brain: The fundamental substrates of human emotions. In H. Corrigall, H. Payne, & I. Wilkinson (Eds.), *About a body: Working with the embodied mind in psychotherapy* (pp. 14–32). Routledge.

Panksepp, J., & Biven, L. (2012). *The archaeology of mind: Neuroevolutionary origins of human emotions*. W. W. Norton.

Porges, S. W. (2011). *The polyvagal theory*. W. W. Norton.

Tronick, E. (2007). *The neurobehavioral and social-emotional development of infants and children*. Norton.

Vingerhoets, A. J. J. M. (2013). *Why only humans weep: Unravelling the mysteries of tears*. Oxford University Press.

Vingerhoets, A. J. J. M., & Bylsma, L. M. (2016). The riddle of human emotional crying: A challenge for emotion researchers. *Emotion Review*, 8(3), 207–217. https://doi.org/10.1177/1754073915586226

Chapter 10

CARE

Allostatic Function of CARE

CARE is the system that is responsible for nurturing and caregiving behaviors. It is particularly important for establishing and maintaining the bond between parents and their offspring that ensures survival. It also influences social bonding and empathy that is needed for social cohesion and individual well-being (Bowlby, 1988).

In Jaak Panksepp's framework of core emotional systems, the CARE system is our brain's ancient, biologically rooted architecture for love, protection, and nurturance (Panksepp, 1998a, 1998b, 2003, 2005a, 2005b, 2006a, 2006b; Panksepp & Biven, 2012). It is what makes a parent stay up all night with a sick child without hesitation, and what draws children into the arms of those who make them feel safe. It is the taproot for social reciprocity that is central to human survival. Without CARE, human parents would simply walk away from their offspring if they felt like it, compete for resources with others in deadly or extremely ruthless ways, and the species would probably not survive. CARE is the essence of empathy as the relationship between child and caregiver creates a shared neurochemistry and sympathetic mirroring of the two beings.

The CARE system is more than a feeling: It is a neural network deeply embedded in the subcortex of the mammalian brain. It evolved to support maternal (and broadly, parental) behaviors that ensure the survival of vulnerable young. But it does more than keep infants alive. It teaches children what safety feels like, what connection means, and what it is to be cared for. Attachment, in this sense, is the first body memory that is later transferred to the self in the form of agency. Those who have had complicated attachment in early life tend to have difficulty with feeling confident about their sense of self. Good attachment tunes the infant's stress-response mechanisms and lays the groundwork for self-regulation and social emotional resilience and weak attachment creates dysregulation of the stress system and the limbic system (Tronick, 2007). Safe attachment also evokes the ventral vagus complex and the parasympathetic nervous system which is responsible for the calm, rest, and digest state that is essential for the body to balance sympathetic energy depletion (Porges, 2011).

DOI: 10.4324/9781003745686-12

Neurobiologically, this system is powered by oxytocin, prolactin, and endogenous opioids which are three neurochemicals that work together to support bonding, caregiving, and emotional regulation, particularly in early development. Oxytocin facilitates trust, eye contact, and physical closeness, and plays a key role in labor, breastfeeding, and parent-infant attachment. Prolactin, primarily known for its role in milk production, also enhances parental responsiveness and the emotional motivation to care for young. Endogenous opioids, the brain's natural painkillers, are released during affectionate touch and social closeness, providing a sense of calm and reward that reinforces caregiving behaviors (Kolb & Whishaw, 2020). Together, these neurochemicals anchor the CARE system, creating a biological foundation for safety, soothing, and secure attachment between child and caregiver. When a caregiver hears their infant cry and rushes to soothe them, this system is firing. It is also active when a child is gently rocked, when eye contact is sustained during feeding, and even when a teacher instinctively crouches to comfort a distressed student.

The brain regions involved, the anterior cingulate cortex (ACC), the periaqueductal gray (PAG), and the ventromedial hypothalamus, are not part of the conscious thinking or language areas of brain. This is instinctual caregiving, not calculated parenting. And that is the point: These behaviors unfold naturally, as long as the system is intact, and the environment is supportive. We do not choose to be attached or not when we are babies. In fact, studies of children in orphanages and neglectful environments have shown that when attachment is prevented the human child dies or becomes severely disabled (Baer & Martinez, 2006). Failure to thrive is a real and devastating illustration of the power of attachment and its absence.

Disordered Attachment

Children without consistent access to this caregiving system often struggle with emotion regulation, social relatedness, and even empathy development. Disorders of attachment, trauma-related dysregulation, and callous-unemotional traits all have roots in disrupted CARE circuitry. From a neurodevelopmental lens, secure attachment is not optional rather it is regulatory scaffolding for the brain (very much a bottom-up process). When the CARE system is repeatedly thwarted or absent, the child's nervous system becomes organized around survival, not connection. This rewiring is adaptive in the short term but costly in the long term, setting the stage for emotional dysregulation, disrupted relational patterns, and psychiatric vulnerability.

In the absence of safe, attuned relationships, the brain begins to wire itself around threat and repeated trauma (Perry & Pollard, 1998). This has lasting consequences for how the child thinks, feels, learns, and relates to others. Children are born with brains that expect caregiving. They are biologically wired to bond, to seek proximity, and to co-regulate with a calm, present adult. When that caregiving is absent, frightening, or unpredictable, it doesn't just hurt the child emotionally, it changes the way their brain grows.

One of the first structures to respond is the amygdala, the brain's alarm system. In children with early trauma or attachment disruption, it becomes hyperactive, always scanning for danger even when none is present. This leads to chronic anxiety, difficulty calming down, and emotional overreactions to minor stressors. Meanwhile, the hippocampus, responsible for memory and contextual learning, may shrink in volume because stress hormones are toxic to the hippocampus neurons. In turn, the child's ability to make sense of time, events, and consequences is weakened (Tottenham & Sheridan, 2009).

Just as important is the prefrontal cortex, especially the medial regions such as the anterior cingulate, that help us reflect, plan, and manage emotions. Without consistent co-regulation from a caregiver, these areas do not develop efficiently. The result is poor impulse control, limited frustration tolerance, and challenges with empathy and problem-solving. Communication between brain hemispheres, often affected via the corpus callosum, may also be diminished, further impairing emotional integration and language-based expression of feelings (Perry, 2006; Teicher, 2004).

Neurochemically, the child's stress system becomes unbalanced. Cortisol, the primary stress hormone, often remains elevated or erratic, keeping the child in a persistent state of hyperarousal. At the same time, levels of oxytocin (the bonding hormone) are often suppressed, making it difficult for the child to trust or connect with others. Dopamine and serotonin, essential for motivation and mood regulation, may also be affected, contributing to depressive symptoms, irritability, or impulsive behavior (Pansepp & Biven, 2012; Kolb & Whishaw, 2020).

These neurobiological shifts translate into very real, everyday struggles. We see it in the child who lashes out unpredictably, the one who clings desperately then pushes others away, or the one who appears emotionally shut down. These behaviors are not defiance or dysfunction, they are adaptations to a world that has taught the child that connection is not safe, and that needs are dangerous or futile. Therefore, successful trauma therapies focus on bringing the overwhelming experience into conscious awareness where the individual can use the information to identify their emotions and then use them as tools for living.

Physiology and Neuroanatomy of CARE

Panksepp spent a great deal of time examining the CARE system (Panksepp, 1998a, 1998b, 2003, 2005a, 2005b, 2006a, 2006b; Panksepp & Biven, 2012). At the neuroanatomical level, the CARE system is deeply rooted in subcortical and limbic structures. The medial preoptic area of the hypothalamus plays a central role in initiating and sustaining maternal behaviors, especially in response to infant cues such as crying or physical proximity. The PAG in the midbrain contributes to the physical expression of caregiving such as grooming, nursing, and protective behaviors while also regulating pain and distress. The ACC is involved in emotional attunement and social concern, helping parents remain responsive to the needs of their young. In addition, the ventral tegmental area and nucleus accumbens, both part of the brain's reward circuitry, reinforce caregiving by linking nurturing actions to pleasurable affect.

Neurochemically, the CARE system is powered by a suite of hormones and neurotransmitters that promote attachment and soothing. Oxytocin, sometimes referred to as the "bonding hormone", plays a central role in fostering trust, physical closeness, and emotional safety. It is released during birth, lactation, skin-to-skin contact, and during emotionally intimate moments across the lifespan. Prolactin supports maternal readiness and is involved in the physiological processes of caregiving and milk production. The system is further supported by dopamine, which reinforces caregiving behaviors by activating the brain's reward centers, and endogenous opioids, such as beta-endorphins, which promote feelings of comfort and reduce the perception of pain during close social contact.

Physiologically, activation of the CARE system enhances parasympathetic nervous system activity, promoting states of calmness and regulation. This facilitates behavioral synchrony between caregiver and child, including eye contact, vocal prosody, physical attunement, and the soothing effects of touch. These bodily signals not only strengthen the caregiver-infant bond, but also shape the child's developing brain by fostering safety, neuroplasticity, and affective regulation.

Continuum of Expression: CARE

At the foundational level, children thrive when caregiving is warm, responsive, and predictable, helping to establish secure attachment patterns and build trust in others. As children grow, they begin to mirror this care by showing early empathy, supported by the maturing interplay between emotional and cognitive brain systems. In cooperative bonding, CARE becomes mutual and flexible: Children learn not only to seek comfort but also to provide it in age-appropriate ways.

With compassionate autonomy, individuals maintain emotional closeness while expressing independence, reflecting well-regulated neural networks and a balanced autonomic state. Finally, in the generative phase, caregiving becomes an integral part of one's identity extending to family, community, and even pets and reflecting a mature CARE system supported by sustained oxytocin and dopamine pathways. This developmental trajectory highlights how CARE not only fosters relational health but also promotes resilience, leadership, and social harmony.

The Continuum of CARE Expression outlined in Table 10.1 illustrates how the brain's caregiving circuitry can function along a spectrum from healthy, attuned caregiving to dysregulated or disrupted expressions of care. At normative levels, the CARE system supports warm, responsive interactions that foster secure attachment, stress regulation, and empathy. However, when caregiving experiences are inconsistent, overwhelming, or absent, the system may become dysregulated. Mild disruptions might appear as overinvolvement or anxious caregiving, while more significant dysregulation can lead to emotional withdrawal, irritability in caregiving roles, or even role confusion where the child assumes the caregiving role. At the most severe end, individuals may exhibit detachment, inability to nurture others, or caregiving patterns driven by unresolved trauma rather than connection. Each level reflects changes in the neural architecture of the CARE system particularly in circuits involving the ACC, hypothalamus, PAG, and neurochemicals like oxytocin, prolactin, and endogenous opioids. Understanding this continuum allows clinicians, caregivers, and educators to identify where support is needed to restore balance and promote healthier, more adaptive caregiving and emotional connection. Tables 10.1 and 10.2 summarize different perspectives on the continuum of CARE expression.

Cultural Factors

It is important to remember that CARE, like all emotions, is culture bound and may be expressed differently depending on the individual's socioeconomic status, sex, gender, racial, ethnic, ableness, and other cultural factors. The CARE system is biologically designed to foster nurturance, attachment, and social bonding, but its expression, structure, and expectations are shaped by culture. While the neurochemicals underlying CARE such as oxytocin, prolactin, and endogenous opioids are universal, the way caregiving behaviors are practiced, valued, and interpreted differs widely across cultural contexts.

In collectivist cultures, caregiving is often extended beyond the nuclear family to include grandparents, aunts, uncles, and community members. In these contexts, caregiving may be less verbal and more action-based emphasizing responsibility, food preparation, shared labor, or protection rather than overt emotional expression (Strand et al., 2019). This can lead to misinterpretation of attachment security if clinicians expect caregiving to always be affectionate or emotionally demonstrative.

By contrast, individualistic cultures may place more emphasis on verbal affirmation, autonomy-supportive parenting, and psychological attunement. In these settings, children are often encouraged to express needs and emotions directly, and caregiving is sometimes measured

Table 10.1 Continuum of CARE Expression (Positive Developmental Perspective)

Level of CARE	Description	Neural Correlates	Functional Role
1. Foundational CARE	Caregiving is warm, predictable, and responsive; child experiences secure physical and emotional presence	Balanced activity in anterior cingulate cortex (ACC), periaqueductal gray (PAG), and hypothalamus; high oxytocin and endogenous opioid levels	Supports secure attachment, stress resilience, and basic trust in relationships
2. Growing Empathy	Child begins to internalize caregiving values and shows concern for others; early emotional reciprocity emerges	Maturing connectivity between limbic system and prefrontal cortex; oxytocin and prolactin facilitate empathic behaviors	Encourages social learning, emotional literacy, and mutual regulation
3. Cooperative Bonding	Care is mutual and flexible; child can seek comfort and offer care to others in age-appropriate ways	Strong integration between prefrontal cortex, ACC, and brainstem attachment circuits; sustained oxytocin signaling	Promotes teamwork, trust, and complex social navigation

Level of CARE	Description	Neural Correlates	Functional Role
4. Compassionate Autonomy	Individual shows independence while remaining emotionally connected to caregivers and peers; gives and receives care fluidly	Efficient regulation across social-affiliative and cognitive networks; balanced autonomic activity	Fosters resilience, leadership, and compassion in social contexts
5. Generative CARE	Person takes on caregiving roles for others (e.g. siblings, community, pets); caregiving becomes a core identity function	Mature engagement of CARE system pathways; modulation by dopamine and oxytocin in socially rewarding contexts	Strengthens interdependence, community integration, and generativity

by emotional presence and reflective listening. However, this model can pathologize families from other cultural backgrounds who demonstrate love and commitment through more functional or role-based forms of care (Markus & Kitayama, 1991).

Gender roles also strongly shape the CARE system. In many cultures, caregiving is feminized, leading to different expectations, burdens, and emotional access for boys and girls. Male expressions of nurturance may be discouraged or only permitted in specific relational roles (e.g. protector vs. emotional caregiver). This can create internal conflict or shame in individuals whose natural CARE impulses do not align with gendered socialization (Eagly & Wood, 2012).

Socioeconomic and historical context also affect how CARE is enacted. In communities affected by poverty, war, migration, or systemic oppression, caregiving may be organized around survival, discipline, or resilience-building, rather than emotional co-regulation. These adaptations, while protective, can limit the child's access to soothing, attuned caregiving without reflecting a lack of love or commitment (Evans, 2004).

Spiritual and philosophical traditions further shape the CARE system by defining who is worthy of care, how suffering is interpreted, and whether dependence is seen as weakness or part of human interdependence. For example, some Indigenous and Eastern philosophies promote a relational worldview, where caregiving extends to animals, land, and ancestors, broadening the scope of CARE well beyond interpersonal bonding (Kimmerer, 2013).

In clinical work, it is critical not to universalize any single model of attachment or caregiving. CARE is always culturally expressed, and expressions of empathy, nurturance, or parenting must

Table 10.2 Continuum of CARE Expression from Secure to Shutdown

Level	Description	Neural Correlates	Functional Role
1. Secure Nurturance	Warm, attuned, and consistent caregiving; emotional availability; ability to give and receive care in developmentally appropriate ways	Balanced activity in the anterior cingulate cortex (ACC), periaqueductal gray (PAG), and hypothalamus; robust oxytocin and endogenous opioid signaling	Fosters secure attachment, emotional regulation, and prosocial behavior; builds trust and relational resilience
2. Sensitive but Inconsistent Care	Care is present but unreliable; emotional attunement fluctuates; caregiving may be distracted, anxious, or overinvolved	Variable prefrontal-ACC coupling; modest oxytocin release; mild dysregulation in limbic-hypothalamic pathways	Promotes anxious or ambivalent attachment; increases vigilance and dependency in relationships; some emotional regulation may be present but fragile
3. Detached or Instrumental Care	Caregiving is mechanical, emotionally flat, or task-focused; lacks warmth or mutual enjoyment; touch and empathy may be minimal	Underactivation of PAG and oxytocin pathways; reduced connectivity between limbic and social-affiliative circuits	Fosters avoidant attachment styles; children may appear self-reliant but struggle with intimacy and emotional depth
4. Disrupted or Distorted Care	Care is frightening, chaotic, or abusive; caregiver may be source of fear or neglect; child experiences profound disorganization	Hyperactivation of the amygdala; reduced hippocampal volume; blunted oxytocin response; heightened cortisol release	Leads to disorganized attachment; impairs emotion regulation, trust, and empathy; associated with trauma responses and relational dysregulation

Level	Description	Neural Correlates	Functional Role
5. CARE System Shutdown	Near-total absence of caregiving; chronic deprivation; institutionalization or extreme neglect	Global underactivation of CARE-related circuits; severely blunted oxytocin, dopamine, and endogenous opioid systems	Profound social withdrawal, failure to thrive, or reactive attachment disorder; impaired development of basic relational capacities and emotional integration

be interpreted through the client's social and cultural lens. Without this sensitivity, clinicians risk mislabeling functional caregiving systems as neglectful or lacking in attunement simply because they differ from Western norms.

Practical Translation of CARE

Clients who have a history of early childhood trauma and disruptions in the CARE system are not broken; they are surviving. Every rejection, defiance, or withdrawal is an echo of early caregiving that did not arrive when it was needed. The goal in counseling is to exploit the fact that the brain is plastic and with the right support, the CARE system can be reawakened. It is never too late to offer a child the experience of being seen, soothed, and safe. The Affective Inventory method is designed to boost oxytocin, dopamine, and endogenous opioids through warm interactions, shared laughter, play, and proximity. This form of parallel play provides predictable moments of connection that stimulate the CARE system's healing pathways.

Just as issues with the other core emotions, it is important to have an overall goal if you identify that the CARE system should be the focus of treatment. Knowing the brain anatomy and chemicals that make up the CARE system will help you target things that you can do to stimulate the system. So, if there is a lacking in oxytocin, prolactin etc. then what should the client do to increase these pathways in the brain? We have to work on creating consistent warm relationships with others. For those who have had disruptions in early childhood this will take a long time. For others who have been isolating themselves or have less severe attachment issues, the same principles apply. The goal for the counselor is to first establish the safe warm relationship with the child and then draw others in to transfer the security into everyday life. If parents are untenable then perhaps an extended family member can step in. Group counseling is a good transitional form of work, as is creating situations where the client is paired with other students in projects or play situations. Superficial relationships will not evoke the CARE system and so we have to be imaginative with how we create the support for the child and also help them have the social skills to decide who to trust and get close to. It is very important to rally the principal adult players in the child's life and have them on the same page as to what to do to encourage the child to have a relationship, and perhaps more important, what to do when the child tests the veracity of the relationship (which they will do because they do not trust easily or even know what a trusting relationship feels like). In addition, if all we do is set up the CARE system and do not work with the other emotion tools, we will set the child up to not know how to defend themselves if the relationships do not work out. They must have the whole toolbox to protect these warm but tenuous feelings.

Counseling Goals for CARE (Neurobiological Perspective)

Goal: To support the client in strengthening secure attachment patterns and enhancing empathy, caregiving behaviors, and self-compassion by activating the CARE system and restoring trust in interpersonal safety.

Rationale: The CARE system is foundational to human attachment, nurturing behavior, and social connectedness. Neurochemically, this system is driven primarily by oxytocin, prolactin, and endogenous opioids, all of which promote social bonding, emotional warmth, and protective caregiving instincts. When functioning well, the CARE system fosters prosocial behavior, compassion, and a sense of mutual responsibility.

Neuroanatomically, the CARE system involves the anterior cingulate cortex (ACC), ventromedial hypothalamus, periaqueductal gray (PAG), and nucleus accumbens. These structures are closely linked with affect regulation, reward processing, and autonomic calming. In individuals with early attachment disruptions, trauma, or chronic stress, these circuits may be underactive or entangled with fear and defense systems.

Clinical Application: In counseling, the goal is to gently reactivate the CARE system by creating a relational space marked by safety, attunement, and emotional responsiveness. This might involve modeling compassionate presence, guiding clients in practices of empathy (toward self and others), and exploring moments of emotional connection in daily life. For some clients, especially those with histories of neglect or relational trauma, activating CARE must begin with cautious exposure to trust, connection, and caregiving experiences.

This system also plays a critical role in parenting, peer relationships, and therapeutic alliance. By helping clients identify how they give and receive care, and where that flow has been interrupted, we lay the groundwork for emotional repair and relational empowerment. Over time, cultivating the CARE system helps the client move from self-protection to co-regulation and emotional generosity.

Therapeutic Touchpoints/Goals for CARE in the Affective Inventory Framework

The ideas the client should walk away with:

1. CARE Is a Core Emotional System That Regulates Safety, Connection, and Belonging
   The CARE system is not just a feeling; it is a biologically embedded part of the brain that supports attachment, empathy, and nurturing relationships. It is activated through warm, attuned caregiving and helps create the sense that we are seen, valued, and emotionally safe in the presence of others.
2. Warm, Predictable Relationships Are a Biological Necessity Not a Luxury
   CARE is as essential to development as food or sleep. Children (and adults) need consistent emotional presence and nurturing touch to feel safe and regulated. This is not a sign of weakness; it is how the human nervous system is designed. Without access to safe caregiving, the stress system dominates, and the brain is shaped for survival rather than connection.

3 Disruptions in CARE Lead to Emotional and Social Dysregulation but the System Can Be Reawakened
When caregiving is inconsistent, absent, or frightening, the brain begins to wire around mistrust, hypervigilance, or withdrawal. These adaptations are protective, not pathological. With the right conditions such as warmth, predictability, and attunement, the CARE system can recover, and trust can be rebuilt over time.
4 CARE Is About Co-Regulation First Then Self-Regulation
We don't learn to calm ourselves in isolation. Children first borrow the nervous systems of calm, present adults, and eventually internalize that safety. For clients who never had that experience, therapy becomes a space where co-regulation can happen safely and consistently until the client can do it for themselves.
5 CARE Is Neurochemical We Can Influence It on Purpose
Oxytocin, prolactin, and endogenous opioids are the core neurochemicals behind CARE. These can be boosted through affectionate touch, eye contact, laughter, warm tone of voice, shared meals, rocking, holding, and emotional attunement. Clients should be encouraged to actively practice CARE behaviors with trusted others to reinforce the system's neural pathways.
6 Empathy, Connection, and Compassion Are Learned Skills
Some clients worry that they are "bad at relationships" or lack empathy. Often, these deficits are not fixed traits but the result of developmental gaps. With modeling, emotional education, and consistent care, even individuals with deep attachment wounds can learn to form meaningful, reciprocal relationships.
7 The Goal Is Internalized Safety and Relational Flexibility
CARE is about more than closeness: It is about developing a nervous system that knows how to trust, reach out, and receive help without fear or shame. Clients should be supported in forming secure, flexible relationships that allow for closeness and autonomy. Over time, this becomes the foundation for leadership, parenting, and prosocial engagement in the world.
8 CARE Must Be Culturally Informed and Developmentally Appropriate
CARE is expressed differently across cultures, genders, and developmental stages. What feels nurturing to one person may feel invasive or inadequate to another. Therapy should help clients explore what CARE looks like for them, honor cultural frameworks, and define new relational patterns that feel authentic and safe.

Client Handout 6: The CARE System: Your Brain's Way of Helping You Feel Close and Connected

Client Handout 6: CARE System	Description
What Is CARE?	It is your brain's "I care about you" system. It makes you want to help, protect, and be kind to people or pets you love
How Can I Tell It Is On?	You feel warm, gentle, or protective, like when you want to hug someone, help a friend, or care for an animal
Why Is It So Important?	CARE helps us build strong relationships. It teaches us empathy, trust, and kindness. It helps us feel safe and loved
What Turns It Off?	Being hurt, ignored, or feeling unsafe can make CARE shut down. You might feel cold, distant, or like you want to pull away
How Do We Turn It Back On?	Do something kind. Hug someone, help a friend, or care for a pet. Being around people who care about you helps, too
Is Empathy Part of CARE?	Yes! Empathy, feeling what someone else feels, is a big part of CARE. It helps us connect with others and understand their needs
What Helps It Work Best?	Feeling safe and loved helps CARE grow. When people show us kindness, our brains learn to do the same for others
Can It Get Confused?	Sometimes. If someone hurts us but also shows care, it can be confusing. Counseling helps us sort that out and learn healthy caring
What If I've Lost It?	It can come back. When we feel safe, accepted, and supported, the CARE system can grow again, even after hard times
Why Does It Matter in Counseling?	CARE helps build trust between you and your therapist. It also helps you learn to care for yourself and others in healthy ways

In addition, here are some ideas for questions that can help the client incorporate the ideas about the emotion into their everyday life:

Client Reflection Handout: My CARE System

1. When do you feel like helping or taking care of someone?

2. What's one kind thing you did recently?

3. Describe a time when someone showed you care or support.

4. Who makes you feel safe, loved, or cared for?

5. What's one way you can show care for yourself or someone else this week?

Draw Your CARE Self!
Use the space below to draw what your CARE system looks like when it is working. You can draw yourself giving a hug, helping someone, or feeling warm and kind inside.

Note: A downloadable version of this handout is available via the webpage for the book at: www.routledge.com/9781041250135

References

Baer, J. C., & Martinez, C. D. (2006). Child maltreatment and insecure attachment: A meta-analysis. *Journal of Reproductive and Infant Psychology*, 24(3), 187–197. https://doi.org/10.1080/02646830600821231

Bowlby, J. (1988). *A secure base: Parent-Child attachment and healthy human development*. Basic Books.

Eagly, A. H., & Wood, W. (2012). Social role theory. In In P. A. M. Van Lange, A. W. Kruglanski, & Van Lange, P. A. M., Kruglanski, A. W., & Higgins, E. T. (Eds.). (2012). *Handbook of theories of social psychology* (pp. 458–476). Sage.

Evans, G. W. (2004). The environment of childhood poverty. *American Psychologist*, 59(2), 77–92.

Kolb, B., & Whishaw, I. (2020). *Fundamentals of human neuroscience* (8th ed.). Worth.

Kimmerer, R. W. (2013). *Braiding sweetgrass*. Milkweed Editions.

Markus, H. R., & Kitayama, S. (1991). Culture and the self: Implications for cognition, emotion, and motivation. *Psychological Review*, 98(2), 224–253.

Panksepp, J. (1998a). *Affective neuroscience: The foundations of human and animal emotions*. Oxford University Press.

Panksepp, J. (1998b). The periconscious substrates of consciousness: Affective states and the evolutionary origins of the SELF. *Journal of Consciousness Studies*, 5(5–6), 566–582.

Panksepp, J. (2003). At the interface between the affective, behavioral, and cognitive neurosciences: Decoding the emotional feelings of the brain. *Brain and Cognition*, 52(1), 4–14.

Panksepp, J. (2005a). Affective consciousness: Core emotional feelings in animals and humans. *Consciousness and Cognition*, 14(1), 30–80.

Panksepp, J. (2005b). On the embodied neural nature of the core emotional affects. *Journal of Consciousness Studies*, 12(8–10), 158–184.

Panksepp, J. (2006a). Emotional endophenotypes in evolutionary psychiatry. *Progress in Neuro-Psychopharmacology & Biological Psychiatry*, 30(5), 774–784.

Panksepp, J. (2006b). The core emotional systems of the mammalian brain: The fundamental substrates of human emotions. In H. Corrigall, H. Payne, & I. Wilkinson (Eds.), *About a body: Working with the embodied mind in psychotherapy* (pp. 14–32). Routledge.

Panksepp, J., & Biven, L. (2012). *The archaeology of mind: Neuroevolutionary origins of human emotions*. W. W. Norton.

Perry, B. D. (2006). Applying principles of neurodevelopment to clinical work with maltreated and traumatized children. In N. B. Webb (Ed.), *Working with traumatized youth in child welfare* (pp. 27–52). Guilford Press.

Perry, B. D., & Pollard, R. A. (1998). Homeostasis, stress, trauma, and adaptation: A neurodevelopmental view of childhood trauma. *Child and Adolescent Psychiatric Clinics of North America*, 7(1), 33–51.

Porges, S. W. (2011). *The polyvagal theory: Neurophysiological foundations of emotions, attachment, communication, and self-regulation*. Norton.

Strand, P. S., Vossen J. J, & Savage, E. (2019). Culture and child attachment patterns: A behavioral systems synthesis. *Perspectives in Behavioral Science*, 42(4), 835–850.

Teicher, M. H. Dumont, N.L., Vaituzis, C., Giedd, J.N. & Andersen, S.L. (2004). Childhood neglect is associated with reduced corpus callosum area. *Biological Psychiatry*, 56(2), 80–85.

Tottenham, N., & Sheridan, M. A. (2009). A review of adversity, the amygdala and the hippocampus: A consideration of developmental timing. *Frontiers in Human Neuroscience*, 3, 68.

Tronick, E. (2007). *The neurobehavioral and social-emotional development of infants and children*. Norton.

Chapter 11

SCARED (FEAR/ANXIETY)

Note: The continuum of expression of the FEAR/ANXIETY system is quite wide therefore the following chapter will use the more child-friendly term of SCARED to encompass the range. However, it is suggested that clinicians use the SCARED/FEAR/ANXIETY terms appropriate for the client.

Allostatic Function of SCARED

Fear and anxiety are both core emotional tools, but they arise from distinct neural processes and serve different functional roles. Fear is an immediate reaction to a present, identifiable threat. It is rooted in deep, evolutionarily ancient brain structures that trigger rapid responses such as fight, flight, or freeze to ensure survival. This response is automatic, often reflexive, and tightly linked to specific external stimuli. When danger is clear and present, the body mobilizes energy, sharpens attention, and prepares to act. In contrast, anxiety is a more diffuse, anticipatory state. It emerges when the threat is not immediate or clearly defined, but rather imagined, remembered, or expected. Instead of preparing the body for quick action, anxiety heightens vigilance, scanning for potential dangers. It reflects an internal prediction that something could go wrong, even in the absence of direct cues. The body remains on alert, and mental resources are drawn toward evaluating uncertainty and maintaining internal balance.

From one perspective, anxiety is seen as a prolongation or misfiring of fear circuitry, as an unresolved alertness to possible danger. From another, it is viewed as a response to predicted imbalances within the body's internal state, signaling a mismatch between what the brain expects and what it senses. In this way, anxiety functions as a forward-looking emotional signal warning us of potential disruption, whether external or internal, and prompting preemptive action or caution.

Physiology and Neuroanatomical Features of SCARED

Fear and anxiety might feel similar in the body, but they come from different emotional systems in the brain, and they serve different purposes. Fear shows up when there's a clear and present danger. It is fast, automatic, and rooted in deep, ancient brain circuits that help us survive. When

DOI: 10.4324/9781003745686-13

something threatens us, such as a loud noise or a sudden movement, the amygdala kicks into gear. It quickly sends signals to the periaqueductal gray (PAG), a part of the brainstem that tells the body to fight, flee, or freeze. The hypothalamus then triggers a chain reaction: heart rate goes up, pupils dilate, and the body gets ready for action. Neurochemicals like glutamate and norepinephrine rev things up, while GABA tries to keep the system from going into overdrive. Hormones like corticotropin-releasing hormone (CRH)and adrenocorticotropic hormone activate the adrenal glands to release cortisol, giving the body an energy boost to handle the immediate threat (Kolb & Whishaw, 2015; Ledoux & Pine, 2016; Perusini & Fanselow, 2015).

Anxiety, on the other hand, is more about anticipation. It is what happens when we *think* something might go wrong, even if nothing bad is happening right now. It is a slower, more sustained process that involves parts of the brain that track our internal states and memories. The bed nucleus of the stria terminalis (BNST) keeps the system on alert when the danger is vague or unpredictable. The insula monitors what's going on inside the body such as heart rate, gut tension, or tightness in the chest, and helps us interpret those signals (Craig, 2009). Meanwhile, the medial prefrontal cortex (mPFC) and the anterior cingulate are busy predicting what *could* go wrong and trying to prepare for it. The hippocampus adds context from past experiences, especially if we've been through stress or trauma before. Chemically, anxiety involves a different balance of more serotonin and dopamine, along with cortisol and inflammatory signals that can wear on both the brain and the body over time (LeDoux & Pine, 2016).

So, in short: fear is the body's reflexive, in-the-moment reaction to danger, while anxiety is more of a future-focused state that tries to predict and prepare for what *might* happen. Fear helps us survive immediate threats. Anxiety helps us stay vigilant, but when it goes too far, it can lead to exhaustion, tension, and a feeling of being stuck in overdrive. Both are crucial to survival, but they differ in timing, trigger, and the kind of action they call forth.

Continuum of Anxiety/Fear Expression

Fear and anxiety are not isolated emotional events; they are part of a continuum of defensive arousal that spans from brief, adaptive responses to chronic, dysregulated states. This continuum reflects the interplay between bottom-up subcortical systems (primarily the amygdala, PAG, and BNST and top-down regulatory circuits within the mPFC, anterior cingulate cortex, and insular cortex (LeDoux & Pine, 2016; Robinson et al., 2019; Shin & Liberzon, 2010). How these systems communicate determines whether fear and anxiety support adaptive behavior or give rise to psychopathology.

At the lower end of the continuum is context-appropriate, phasic fear: an immediate, time-limited response to an identifiable threat. This level of defensive arousal is mediated by rapid activation of the central nucleus of the amygdala and the dorsal PAG, which mobilize the body for fight, flight, or freeze responses (Mobbs et al., 2015; Phelps & LeDoux, 2005; Tovote et al., 2015). This form of fear is evolutionarily advantageous. It heightens sensory processing, sharpens attention, and prepares the organism for action. Once the threat subsides, the system typically deactivates, allowing the individual to return to a regulated baseline.

Slightly higher on the continuum is anticipatory anxiety, which emerges in the face of uncertain or ambiguous threats. Unlike fear, which is triggered by clearly present danger, anxiety reflects a sustained state of hypervigilance, often with no immediate source of threat. This state is primarily supported by the BNST, which maintains arousal and worry in the absence of specific stimuli (Alvarez et al., 2011; Avery et al., 2016; Davis & Walker, 2014). During this phase, individuals may experience physiological activation, restlessness, or intrusive worry, but are still generally able to engage in goal-directed behavior. Functional imaging typically reveals increased activity in the anterior insula and midcingulate cortex, which track internal bodily states and anticipate aversive outcomes (Paulus & Stein, 2006; Robinson et al., 2019).

As the continuum progresses, anxiety may become generalized and pervasive, characterized by chronic overactivation of threat-detection systems and impaired prefrontal modulation. This state often reflects disruptions in the connectivity between the amygdala and prefrontal cortex, as well as heightened sensitivity in the default mode network, which promotes excessive self-referential thought and rumination (LeDoux & Pine, 2016; Shin & Liberzon, 2010). At this level, individuals report persistent unease, somatic tension, impaired concentration, and avoidance behaviors. These symptoms are no longer merely adaptive; they interfere with functioning and reduce cognitive flexibility.

At the upper end of the continuum is panic and traumatic re-experiencing, in which fear responses become dysregulated and intrusive, often occurring without external triggers. Panic states are associated with acute surges of sympathetic arousal involving the PAG, locus coeruleus, and hypothalamus, as well as dysfunctional feedback loops between the ventromedial prefrontal cortex and limbic regions (Mobbs et al., 2015; Pitman et al., 2012; Shin & Liberzon, 2010). In posttraumatic states, fear memories may be improperly consolidated, leading to flashbacks, exaggerated startle responses, and avoidance behaviors that further entrench the dysregulation (Pitman et al., 2012).

Throughout this continuum, the functional role of fear and anxiety remains rooted in survival. However, what determines whether these states are adaptive or pathological is not simply the presence of arousal, but the degree of modulation, context sensitivity, and recovery capacity. In healthy individuals, fear and anxiety are transient and proportionate to threat. In dysregulated states, they become decoupled from external reality, overly persistent, and resistant to top-down control (LeDoux & Pine, 2016; Shin & Liberzon, 2010).

The Continuum of Anxiety and Fear Expression outlined in Table 11.1 shows fear-based responses develop and shift along a spectrum from adaptive, protective functions to maladaptive patterns that interfere with functioning. At the normal end, brief and proportionate fear or anxiety responses serve important survival functions such as alerting us to danger and helping us prepare for future threats. These responses are typically mediated by the amygdala, hypothalamus, and PAG, and are modulated by neurochemicals like norepinephrine and cortisol.

As fear and anxiety become more persistent or exaggerated, individuals may experience heightened vigilance, intrusive worry, or avoidance behaviors. These moderate expressions often reflect increased limbic activation with less regulatory input from the prefrontal cortex. In more severe cases, such as chronic anxiety or trauma-related disorders, fear circuitry may become dysregulated leading to overwhelming panic, dissociation, or learned helplessness. At this end of the spectrum, neuroplastic changes may reinforce maladaptive pathways, making fear responses more automatic and difficult to inhibit (LeDoux & Pine, 2016; Robinson et al., 2019; Shin & Liberzon, 2010). By viewing fear and anxiety on a continuum we gain a deeper appreciation for how these emotional systems function protectively and how interventions can be tailored to restore safety, flexibility, and cognitive-emotional integration.

Cultural Factors

It is important to remember that SCARED, like all emotions, is culture bound and may be expressed differently depending on the individual's socioeconomic status, sex, gender, racial, ethnic, ableness, and other cultural factors. Different cultures teach individuals what is considered threatening, what should be feared, and how fear should be handled. For example, in collectivist societies, fear may center around social disruption, shame, or dishonoring the group, whereas in individualistic cultures, it may relate more to personal failure, loss of autonomy, or humiliation. These culturally shaped fears activate the same biological circuitry but differ in psychological content and behavioral expression (Kitayama et al., 2006; Mesquita & Walker, 2003).

Table 11.1 Continuum of Anxiety and Fear Expression

Level	Description	Neural Correlates	Functional Role
1. Alert Readiness	Mild vigilance in response to novelty or uncertainty	Moderate activation of amygdala, locus coeruleus, and anterior insula; intact prefrontal regulation	Promotes exploration and situational awareness
2. Anticipatory Anxiety	Future-oriented worry with physiological arousal	Increased amygdala and bed nucleus of the stria terminalis (BNST) activity; HPA axis mildly activated	Encourages planning and avoidance of potential threats
3. Situational Fear	Acute fear in response to specific stimuli or threats	Surge in amygdala and periaqueductal gray (PAG) activity; sympathetic nervous system arousal	Triggers fight, flight, or freeze to ensure survival
4. Generalized Anxiety/ Hypervigilance	Persistent worry and scanning for danger across contexts	Chronic amygdala hyperactivity, medial prefrontal cortex (mPFC) underactivation, dysregulated HPA axis	Maladaptive; interferes with daily functioning and learning
5. Panic or Phobic Reactivity	Intense, often irrational, fear responses to specific cues	Overactivation of limbic system, insula, PAG; reduced prefrontal inhibition	May lead to phobic avoidance and social withdrawal

Level	Description	Neural Correlates	Functional Role
6. Pathological Anxiety/Trauma Response	Severe, chronic fear or anxiety often linked to trauma	Disrupted connectivity between amygdala, hippocampus, and prefrontal cortex; HPA axis dysregulation	Compromises executive functioning, memory, and relational safety

Socialization practices also train the nervous system to either suppress or tolerate fear-based emotions. In cultures that value stoicism, emotional restraint, or duty, outward expressions of fear such as trembling, crying, or freezing may be discouraged. Over time, this can increase the likelihood of somatization or dissociation, making fear states harder to identify in clinical encounters (Hinton & Good, 2016; Mesquita & Walker, 2003). In contrast, cultures that encourage more expressive responses may support quicker discharge of autonomic arousal, especially when paired with social co-regulation.

Historical trauma and intergenerational threat exposure also leave epigenetic and behavioral imprints on the SCARED system. For individuals who live within marginalized communities, refugee populations, Indigenous groups, or communities exposed to systemic violence, the SCARED system may become chronically sensitized even in the absence of immediate danger. Hypervigilance, shutdown, or mistrust of authority are not overreactions, they are adaptive responses to a historically hostile environment (Kirmayer et al., 2014; Yehuda & Lehrner, 2018).

Trauma and PTSD

Posttraumatic stress disorder (PTSD) is not simply a problem of memory. It is a full-body, full-brain condition rooted in survival. Healing requires more than remembering or retelling what happened: It requires the restoration of internal regulation, safety, and emotional connection which are all biologically based states. Trauma overwhelms our deepest emotional and physiological systems. These systems normally work in concert to help us make sense of our environment and to maintain a coherent sense of self. But when terrifying or life-threatening events occur without warning, our nervous system shifts into a defensive mode aimed purely at survival. It does not stop to understand or contextualize what is happening and so it acts to preserve life in the moment.

According to Panksepp (2006a; Panksepp & Biven, 2012) this survival response is deeply primitive, originating in subcortical regions of the brain that evolved long before our capacity for narrative thought or reflective insight. As a result, trauma disrupts the ability of the prefrontal cortex (responsible for executive function, regulation, and self-awareness) to integrate experience. The brain's more advanced regions go offline until it is safe to re-engage. What remains is a neural imprint which is an enduring state of threat readiness that may later be triggered without conscious awareness.

From the perspective of affective neuroscience (e.g. Panksepp & Biven, 2012), PTSD reflects a state of dysregulation at the upper end of the fear-anxiety continuum. The amygdala, which detects and responds to danger, becomes hyperreactive, while the prefrontal cortex (especially the medial and ventromedial regions) fails to exert sufficient top-down regulation. The hippocampus, critical for encoding context and distinguishing past from present, often shows reduced volume and activity (Pitman et al., 2012). Consequently, traumatic memories may be stored in fragmented, sensory, or emotionally charged forms, rather than integrated into autobiographical memory. The individual is then vulnerable to intrusive re-experiencing, flashbacks, and emotional disorientation (Kolb & Whishaw, 2020).

In addition to these fear-based disruptions, PTSD also involves broader dysregulation of the brain's primary emotional systems, as described by Jaak Panksepp (Panksepp & Biven, 2012). The SADNESS system, responsible for separation distress and loss, may become overactivated, particularly in the context of abandonment, betrayal, or attachment trauma. This can lead to emotional numbing, social withdrawal, and despair. The ANGER system may be sensitized, manifesting as irritability, anger outbursts, or reactive aggression. Meanwhile, the SEEKING system, which ordinarily fuels motivation, curiosity, and social connection, often becomes suppressed, leaving individuals feeling disconnected, inert, or emotionally flat. In this way, trauma impairs not only the individual's ability to regulate fear, but also their capacity to feel joy, purpose, and engagement with the world.

A complementary perspective comes from A. D. (Bud) Craig's work on interoception and emotional prediction. Craig conceptualizes PTSD as a breakdown in the brain's ability to track and interpret the body's internal signals. Under normal conditions, the brain uses interoception to anticipate changes in heart rate, respiration, muscle tension, and other internal states, adjusting them in real time. In trauma, however, this system becomes dysregulated. Everyday bodily sensations, such as a racing heart or a sudden jolt of adrenaline, are misinterpreted as signs of imminent danger. The brain, conditioned by prior trauma, begins to amplify these sensations rather than regulate them. This mismatch between internal perception and external reality creates a persistent state of alarm.

This disruption explains why panic attacks in PTSD can feel so terrifying. The body reacts as if it is under threat, yet the cognitive mind cannot identify any external source. The brain recognizes that something is wrong physiologically, but it cannot make sense of the reaction. This dissociation between body and mind can lead to overwhelming fear, a sense of going crazy, or even the belief that one might die. Over time, these experiences erode one's sense of safety in the world and in oneself, often prompting individuals to seek help for what appear to be unpredictable or irrational symptoms.

In clinical work, it is crucial to understand that these reactions are not irrational at all. They are biologically embedded patterns of protection: deep survival codes that persist long after the danger has passed. Trauma recovery, therefore, must go beyond verbal processing. It must engage the full scope of the brain and body's response system. Interoceptive work, emotional priming, and body-based modalities are essential tools for helping individuals reconnect with their internal states and re-establish accurate emotional signaling. Only then can they begin to revise the narrative of trauma, not as a permanent imprint, but as a chapter in a longer and more coherent story of self.

PTSD thus represents a convergence of dysregulated fear, disrupted interoception, and impaired motivational and emotional systems. It is a disorder of survival mechanisms gone awry and neurobiological state in which the systems designed to protect life inadvertently inhibit living. But with careful, attuned, and multimodal intervention, these systems can be recalibrated. The task of healing is not to erase the trauma, but to restore the capacity for engagement, integration, and hope.

Practical Translation of Trauma/PTSD

Together, the work of Panksepp (Panksepp & Biven, 2012) and Craig (2014) frames trauma not just as a psychological disruption, but as a breakdown in the regulation of ancient emotional circuits and bodily self-awareness. Panksepp provides the emotional architecture: core affective systems that govern fear, loss, anger, and motivation. Craig (2009) offers the sensory scaffolding as the brain's interpretation of internal physiological states that anchor our emotional experience in the body. When trauma strikes, these systems no longer work in harmony. The brain overpredicts threat, the body misinterprets signals, and the emotional circuits that should foster connection and curiosity instead generate fear, withdrawal, or collapse.

Clinically, this integrated view reinforces the need for trauma-informed care that addresses both emotional processing and bodily regulation. Interventions must go beyond cognitive insight. They must include approaches that help recalibrate the SEEKING system, restore interoceptive accuracy, and support the integration of traumatic memory across both brain and body. Healing becomes not simply a matter of retelling the story, but of rewriting the brain's internal scripts, at the level of affective systems and sensory predictions. In doing so, clients can begin to experience safety not only as an idea, but as a felt reality.

Counseling Goal for SCARED (Neurobiological Perspective)

Goal: To help the client recognize, regulate, and gradually recalibrate fear-based emotional responses by increasing interoceptive awareness, enhancing prefrontal engagement, and restoring balance in brain-body circuits associated with fear and anxiety.

Rationale: From a neurochemical standpoint, the FEAR system is driven largely by heightened amygdala activity, with neurochemical contributions from glutamate, corticotropin-releasing factor, and norepinephrine. As stated elsewhere in this chapter, when hyperactive, this system creates persistent vigilance, somatic tension, and hyperarousal. Neuroanatomically, the amygdala and PAG are central in initiating threat responses. In anxiety-prone individuals, regulatory connections from the mPFC and anterior cingulate cortex (ACC) are often under-engaged. These top-down areas are responsible for modulating the primitive threat signals from subcortical structures.

Clinical Application: The therapeutic goal is to help the client build awareness of their physiological fear responses (e.g. tight chest, racing heart), learn to name and map the sensations, and develop techniques to strengthen regulatory circuits (breathwork, paced movement, grounding, cognitive labeling). This strengthens cortico-limbic integration and slowly allows the fear system to recalibrate. The goal is not to suppress fear but to bring it into conscious awareness so it can be used as a guide rather than a command.

Therapeutic Touchpoints/Goals for SCARED in the Affective Inventory Framework

The ideas the client should walk away with:

1. Fear and Anxiety Are Not the Same But Both Are Normal, Adaptive Emotional Systems
   The SCARED system is a hardwired survival mechanism designed to detect and respond to immediate danger (e.g. threat to life or safety). Anxiety, by contrast, is the brain's way of anticipating potential future threats. Both are evolutionarily protective. These responses are not weaknesses because they are evidence that the brain is trying to keep the body safe.
2. SCARED Is Fast and Bottom-Up, It Bypasses Thinking for Speed
   The brain regions that control fear responses, especially the amygdala, PAG, and hypothalamus, are subcortical and not under conscious control. This means fear can be triggered without language, logic, or memory. The body often "knows" something feels wrong before the mind does. Learning to trust and decode those signals is part of emotional literacy.
3. Anxiety Lives in the Future: It Is a Brain Trying to Predict and Prepare
   Anxiety often comes from an overactive prediction system, particularly involving the insula and anterior cingulate cortex. The brain scans for uncertainty and creates "what if" scenarios. Understanding anxiety as the brain's over-preparation can help shift from shame to curiosity: "What is my brain preparing me for, and is it accurate?"
4. Chronic Anxiety Is a Sign of a System That's Been Stuck in Survival Mode
   When the nervous system has been exposed to chronic threat whether due to trauma, unpredictability, or high stress, it begins to organize itself around defense. This can show up as generalized anxiety, phobias, panic attacks, or hypervigilance. The goal is not to eliminate these responses, but to teach the body and brain what "safe enough" feels like again.
5. We Can't Think Our Way Out of SCARED: We Have to Feel Our Way to Safety
   Because fear responses are so fast and primitive, cognitive strategies often don't reach the parts of the brain that are activated during high anxiety. Somatic tools such as breathwork, grounding, sensory regulation, or movement can send safety signals back through the body to the brain. These bottom-up techniques restore access to the prefrontal cortex and support emotional regulation.
6. The Goal Is Not to Eliminate Fear, But to Work with It
   Fear helps us survive. The goal is to be able to notice fear, name it, and choose how to respond rather than be hijacked by it. Clients should learn how to recognize the difference between a real threat and a false alarm and practice choosing grounding responses that give the prefrontal cortex time to re-engage.
7. Predictability and Choice Calm the SCARED System
   Environments that are structured, consistent, and offer real choices help reduce anxiety. This is especially true for children or trauma survivors. Whenever possible, clients should be supported in building routines, increasing their sense of control, and learning to anticipate safe outcomes. Safety is the antidote to fear.
8. Fear and Anxiety Must Be Seen Through a Cultural and Developmental Lens
   What triggers anxiety is shaped by personal history, cultural background, and life experience. Some individuals may express fear through silence, withdrawal, or perfectionism, while others may externalize through agitation or irritability. Therapy should help clients understand their own fear response patterns in a compassionate, culturally informed way.

9 The Nervous System Learns Safety Through Repetition and Relationship
Regulating the SCARED system is not a one-time insight because it needs sustained practice to create new connections. Through repeated safe experiences, the nervous system learns to recalibrate. Trusted relationships, predictable caregiving, and therapeutic attunement allow the fear circuits to relax. Over time, clients build internal cues for "I can handle this" instead of "I need to run".

Because anxiety and fear are reactive and anticipatory in nature and fueled by very powerful neurohormones and chemistry we have much to overcome when trying to assist a client in recovery. We have to go in through the body and get it calmed down for a prolonged period before we can create interventions for the brain-mind. Talk therapy does not work if the body is jacked up on cortisol, adrenaline or stress hormones. An elevated heart rate tells the body it needs resources, and the brain cannot ignore it. Your brain listens to your heart and therefore education about heart rate variability and breathing is critical to therapeutic success. Mindfulness and breathing exercises have been shown to significantly reduce anxiety, but they are not stand-alone methods that lead to insights and therapeutic gains for the long-term. They are very effective methods to get the body calm enough to hear messages and are wonderful tools for life to keep the immune system working well. There is a distinct relationship between stress and lowered immune system functioning opening up the individual for all kinds of chronic illness and autoimmune conditions. Therefore, if SCARED is a part of the client's profile, the *only* way for them to go back to allostasis is through a calm sympathetic nervous system and a responsive parasympathetic nervous system. It is all about balance. Once the body starts to calm, then the Affective Inventory and psychoeducation can do its job.

Client Handout 6: The SCARED System: Your Brain's Built-In Safety Alarm

Client Handout 6: SCARED System	Description
What Is SCARED?	It is your brain's "uh-oh" system. It makes you alert and ready to run, hide, or protect yourself when something feels unsafe
How Can I Tell It Is On?	You might feel jumpy, tense, sweaty, shaky, or like your heart is racing. You may want to freeze, run away, or hide
Why Is It So Important?	FEAR helps you stay safe. It keeps you away from danger. But too much fear can get in the way of doing things you care about. Learning how to calm your body and feel safe again is important for keeping SCARED balanced
What Turns It Off?	Feeling safe, being with people you trust, breathing slowly, or having support can help your brain feel less scared and more calm
How Do We Help It Work Better?	You can talk to someone, practice calming tools (like deep breathing or grounding exercises), and remind yourself that you're safe now. Getting help from a trusted adult or counselor is also really helpful
Is SCARED a Bad Emotion?	No! FEAR is a normal part of being human. It is like an inner smoke alarm; it just needs to be checked to see if the danger is real or not. When it works well, it helps keep us aware and safe
Why Does It Matter in Counseling?	FEAR tells us when something feels too hard or risky. Therapy helps us learn to listen to that feeling, but not let it control us. We learn ways to feel safer, braver, and more in charge

In addition, here are some ideas for questions that can help the client incorporate the ideas about the emotion into their everyday life:

Client Reflection Handout: My SCARED System

1 What kinds of things make you feel scared or nervous?

2 What happens in your body when you feel scared?

3 What helps you calm down when you're feeling afraid?

4 Who do you feel safest with when you're scared?

5 What's one way you've been brave, even when you were scared?

Draw Your SCARED System
Use the space below to draw what your FEAR system looks like. You can draw yourself being scared, calming down, or standing strong with support from others.

Note: A downloadable version of this handout is available via the webpage for the book at: www.routledge.com/9781041250135

References

Alvarez, R. P., Chen, G., Bodurka, J., Kaplan, R., & Grillon, C. (2011). Phasic and sustained fear in humans elicits distinct patterns of brain activity. *NeuroImage*, 55(1), 389–400.

Avery, S. N., Clauss, J. A., & Blackford, J. U. (2016). The human BNST: Functional role in anxiety and addiction. *Neuropsychopharmacology*, 41(1), 126–141.

Craig, A. D. (2009). How do you feel—now? The anterior insula and human awareness. *Nature Reviews Neuroscience*, 10(1), 59–70.

Craig, A. D. (Bud). (2014). *How Do You Feel?: An Interoceptive Moment with Your Neurobiological Self*. Princeton, New Jersey: Princeton University Press.

Davis, M., & Walker, D. L. (2014). Role of bed nucleus of the stria terminalis and amygdala AMPA receptors in the development and expression of context conditioning and sensitization of startle. *Neuropsychopharmacology*, 39(1), 177–187.

Hinton, D. E., & Good, B. J. (2016). *Culture and PTSD: Trauma in global and historical perspective*. University of Pennsylvania Press.

Kirmayer, L. J., Gone, J. P., & Moses, J. (2014). Rethinking historical trauma. *Transcultural Psychiatry*, 51(3), 299–319.

Kitayama, S., Mesquita, B., & Karasawa, M. (2006). Cultural affordances and emotional experience: Socially engaging and disengaging emotions in Japan and the United States. *Journal of Personality and Social Psychology*, 91(5), 890–903.

Kolb, B., & Whishaw, I. Q. (2015). *An introduction to brain and behavior* (4th ed.). Worth Publishers.

Kolb, B., & Whishaw, I. Q. (2020). *Fundamentals of human neuropsychology* (8th ed.). Worth Publishers.

LeDoux, J. E., & Pine, D. S. (2016). Using neuroscience to help understand fear and anxiety: A two-system framework. *American Journal of Psychiatry*, 173(11), 1083–1093.

Mesquita, B., & Walker, R. (2003). Cultural differences in emotions: A context for interpreting emotional experiences. *Behaviour Research and Therapy*, 41(7), 777–793.

Mobbs, D., Hagan, C. C., Dalgleish, T., Silston, B., & Prévost, C. (2015). The ecology of human fear: Survival optimization and the nervous system. *Frontiers in Neuroscience*, 9, 55.

Panksepp, J. (2006a). Emotional endophenotypes in evolutionary psychiatry. *Progress in Neuro-Psychopharmacology & Biological Psychiatry*, 30(5), 774–784.

Panksepp, J., & Biven, L. (2012). *The archaeology of mind: Neuroevolutionary origins of human emotions*. W. W. Norton.

Paulus, M. P., & Stein, M. B. (2006). An insular view of anxiety. *Biological Psychiatry*, 60(4), 383–387. https://doi.org/10.1016/j.biopsych.2006.03.042

Perusini, J. N., & Fanselow, M. S. (2015). Neurobehavioral perspectives on the distinction between fear and anxiety. *Learning and Memory*, 22(9):417–25.

Phelps, E. A., & LeDoux, J. E. (2005). Contributions of the amygdala to emotion processing: From animal models to human behavior. *Neuron*, 48(2), 175–187.

Pitman, R. K., Rasmusson, A. M., Koenen, K. C., Shin, L. M., Orr, S. P., Gilbertson, M. W., Milad, M. R., & Liberzon, I. (2012). Biological studies of post-traumatic stress disorder. *Nature Reviews Neuroscience*, 13(11), 769–787.

Robinson, O. J., Pike, A. C., Cornwell, B., & Grillon, C. (2019). The translational neural circuitry of anxiety. *Journal of Neurology, Neurosurgery & Psychiatry*, 90(12), 1358–1366. https://doi.org/10.1136/jnnp-2019-321400

Shin, L. M., & Liberzon, I. (2010). The neurocircuitry of fear, stress, and anxiety disorders. *Neuropsychopharmacology*, 35(1), 169–191. https://doi.org/10.1038/npp.2009.83

Tovote, P., Fadok, J. P., & Lüthi, A. (2015). Neuronal circuits for fear and anxiety. *Nature Reviews Neuroscience*, 16(6), 317–331. https://doi.org/10.1038/nrn3945

Yehuda, R., & Lehrner, A. (2018). Intergenerational transmission of trauma effects: Putative role of epigenetic mechanisms. *World Psychiatry*, 17(3), 243–257.

Chapter 12

LUST

LUST is one of the brain's primary emotional systems, responsible for sexual feelings and reproductive motivation. In Jaak Panksepp's affective neuroscience model, LUST is far more than a basic sex drive, it is a biologically embedded emotional network that supports intimacy, pair bonding, and the emotional layers of sexual interaction. While society often reduces sexuality to hormones or instinct, LUST is part of a deeply interconnected neurobiological system that links pleasure, identity, and attachment throughout the lifespan.

Allostatic Function of LUST

At its core, the LUST system evolved to facilitate reproduction, ensuring the survival of the species. But its influence extends well beyond mating. It helps shape attraction, relational closeness, and emotional vulnerability, creating a neurological pull toward others that often becomes the foundation for long-term bonds. When healthy, this system supports sexual well-being, intimate connection, and a coherent sense of self. When disrupted through early trauma, cultural shame, repression, or neurodevelopmental differences it can manifest as sexual avoidance, compulsivity, fear, or identity confusion.

Physiology and Neuroanatomical Features of Lust

Neurochemically, LUST is driven by a quartet of interacting hormones and neurotransmitters: testosterone, estrogen, dopamine, and oxytocin. Testosterone energizes sexual motivation and assertiveness across all sexes, while estrogen helps modulate sexual receptivity, pleasure sensitivity, and emotional openness. Dopamine provides the excitement and reward anticipation of LUST while oxytocin promotes intimacy, trust, and bonding during and after sexual contact. Together, these chemicals do more than generate LUST; they help transform sex into an emotionally significant experience (Panksepp & Biven, 2012).

Panksepp described sex differences in the LUST system as hormonally mediated variations in motivation and expression layered onto a shared mammalian circuit, with human experience

DOI: 10.4324/9781003745686-14

powerfully shaped by development, culture, and relational context. Therefore, observed sex differences in adults often reflect developmental shaping layered onto biology, not biology alone.

The brain regions that coordinate these processes include the medial preoptic area (MPOA) and ventromedial hypothalamus both of which are central to initiating and coordinating sexual behavior. The nucleus accumbens, part of the brain's reward system, helps link sexual LUST to pleasurable reinforcement, while the periaqueductal gray (PAG) integrates bodily and emotional aspects of arousal and responsiveness. These subcortical structures operate largely beneath conscious awareness. From a neurochemical perspective, testosterone fuels sexual initiative and interest; estrogen supports responsiveness and bonding; dopamine amplifies anticipation and novelty-seeking; and oxytocin reinforces emotional closeness and trust. These systems are further modulated by cortisol (the stress hormone) and endogenous opioids, which help determine whether sexual touch is soothing or dysregulating. Sexual LUST, like hunger or fear, is not something we necessarily choose because it emerges from neural circuits that are both ancient and powerful (Panksepp, 1998, 2005; Panksepp & Biven, 2012).

Continuum of Expression of LUST

Importantly, the LUST system does not function in isolation from the rest of the emotional brain. It is shaped by early relational experiences, bodily cues, cultural narratives, and attachment patterns. Safe touch, trust, and consistent caregiving in childhood create a neural template for later sexual safety and emotional closeness. Conversely, experiences of neglect, boundary violations, or shame, especially those involving the body or gender identity, can leave lasting imprints on this system. Insecure attachment, particularly when caregiving is inconsistent or emotionally absent, can profoundly affect a person's ability to experience sexual intimacy without fear, ambivalence, or emotional detachment.

When the LUST system is dysregulated or underdeveloped, its expression may become distorted. Some individuals feel anxious, ashamed, or disconnected from their sexual selves, struggling with consent, bodily awareness, or emotional intimacy. Others may turn to compulsive sexual behavior as a coping mechanism for unmet emotional needs. Dysregulation may stem from personal trauma or from broader social factors such as restrictive gender roles, religious teachings, or cultural silencing of sexual expression. In adolescents or adults with trauma histories, sexual arousal may even be misinterpreted by the brain as danger, activating defensive systems rather than pleasure circuits. This can lead to dissociation, panic, or avoidance of intimacy altogether. Table 12.1 summarizes this continuum.

Clinically, it is essential to understand that the LUST system is not just about behavior, it is part of a broader emotional and developmental process. Healing this system requires emotional safety, body-based integration, and attention to the ways in which early life experiences shape adult sexual identity and expression. LUST is not just about sex. It is about the brain's capacity for embodied connection, reward, and emotional intimacy.

Counseling Goals for LUST (Neurobiological Perspective)

Goal: To help the client develop a healthy, embodied understanding of sexual LUST, intimacy, and relational boundaries by fostering awareness of the LUST system's biological foundations and its connection to identity, safety, and human connection.

Rationale: The LUST system, from an affective neuroscience perspective, is not simply about sexual behavior; it is an evolutionarily conserved emotional system that motivates bonding, reproductive behavior, and intimate connection. Neurochemically, the LUST system is influenced

Table 12.1 Continuum of LUST Expression—Dysregulated to Integrated

Level	Description	Neural Correlates	Functional Role
Healthy Integration	Sexuality is experienced as safe, integrated with identity, and connected to emotional intimacy and consent	Balanced activation in MPOA, nucleus accumbens, and oxytocin-dopamine circuits; coordinated limbic-cortical regulation	Promotes well-being, secure bonding, and adult intimacy; supports positive self-esteem and trust in relationships
Anxious or Shame-Based Sexuality	Sexuality is associated with guilt, embarrassment, or anxious rumination; may avoid or overcompensate for discomfort	Fluctuating oxytocin and cortisol activity; increased prefrontal inhibition of limbic reward circuits	Undermines spontaneous sexual expression; may result in conflicted behaviors, relational distance, or compulsivity
Disinhibited or Compulsive Sexuality	Sexual behavior is pursued impulsively, often without emotional connection or clear boundaries	Hyperactivation of mesolimbic dopamine system; reduced prefrontal inhibition and altered serotonin function	Reinforces risky behavior, relational instability, and possible trauma reenactment; may impair intimacy
Fear or Avoidance of Sexuality	Sexual cues elicit fear, shutdown, or dissociation; touch or LUST may be interpreted as threatening	Amygdala hyperactivation; suppressed MPOA and oxytocin pathways; elevated cortisol response	Impairs capacity for trust and sexual safety; often linked to trauma, boundary violations, or cultural conditioning

Level	Description	Neural Correlates	Functional Role
LUST System Shutdown	Sexuality is absent or repressed; individual may feel numb, disconnected from body, or averse to sexual identity	Blunted activity in hypothalamic-limbic circuits; reduced testosterone/ estrogen signaling; diminished dopamine response	Contributes to relational detachment, affective flattening, and identity confusion; often associated with severe neglect, trauma, or depression

by testosterone, estrogen, oxytocin, and dopamine, which work together to support arousal, sexual motivation, and the affective pull toward closeness. Neuroanatomically, the LUST system is centered in hypothalamic regions (particularly the MPOA), the PAG, amygdala, and ventral striatum. These areas coordinate physiological arousal, drive, and affective salience of potential partners. When this system is dysregulated due to trauma, shame, cultural suppression, or overstimulation it can result in confusion, avoidance, compulsion, or detachment from one's own bodily cues (Panksepp & Biven, 2012).

Clinical Application: The therapeutic goal is to create a respectful, developmentally appropriate space for the client to explore how they experience LUST, connection, and bodily pleasure. For adolescents and adults alike, this may involve naming sensations, unpacking social and cultural messages, and exploring how the LUST system overlaps with attachment, safety, and autonomy.

The counselor's task is not to moralize, but to support embodied self-awareness and a respectful, affirming relationship with one's sexual self. This includes clarifying personal boundaries, recognizing when LUST feels safe or unsafe, and understanding how arousal states are linked to brain-body systems, not just cognitive intention.

Ultimately, the goal is to reduce shame, increase self-trust, and integrate the LUST system with the client's broader emotional, relational, and identity development. In doing so, we reframe sexuality not as a problem to control, but as a vital, biologically based emotional system which, when honored and integrated, can enrich human connection and self-understanding.

Therapeutic Touchpoints/Goals for LUST in the Affective Inventory Framework

The ideas the client should walk away with:

1. LUST Is a Core Emotional System, Not Just a Physical Urge
The LUST for closeness, touch, and sexual expression is biologically wired into all humans. This drive is not shameful or inappropriate because it is a core feature of our emotional architecture that evolved to support bonding, reproduction, and intimacy. When understood and integrated, LUST contributes to joy, self-esteem, and healthy relationships.
2. Healthy Sexuality Is Rooted in Safety, Consent, and Connection
The LUST system functions optimally when individuals feel physically safe, emotionally connected, and empowered to set boundaries. Therapy should help clients reconnect with their bodies, restore trust in touch, and identify what safety feels like during closeness. For many, this includes redefining pleasure on their own terms, rather than based on others' expectations.
3. Trauma, Repression, and Shame Can Disrupt the LUST System: But Healing Is Possible
If sexual behavior feels compulsive, disconnected, numb, or frightening, this is not a character flaw it is a signal that the LUST system may have been affected by early experience, trauma, or cultural messaging. The good news is that this system is neuroplastic and can be reshaped through safe relationships, body-based work, and reattuned emotional experiences.
4. Sexual Development Is Interpersonal and Cultural
Cultural norms, religious teachings, and early messages about the body all influence how the LUST system develops. Therapy should explore how these beliefs may have shaped the client's current experience of sexuality and whether they support or hinder self-acceptance, pleasure, and emotional intimacy.
5. Pleasure Is a Regulatory Tool, not a Problem
Sexual pleasure, when experienced safely and consensually, helps regulate the nervous system through the release of oxytocin, dopamine, and endogenous opioids. It calms the body, deepens connection, and enhances emotional vitality. Clients should be encouraged to explore what kinds of touch, connection, or fantasy feel good and safe.
6. The Goal Is Integration, Not Performance
Therapy should not aim to "normalize" sexual behavior or pressure clients into any kind of sexual expression. Instead, it should support the client's ability to feel connected to their body, identify their own LUSTs and limits, and form relationships based on mutual respect and attunement. Integration means that sexuality becomes one part of the self not a secret, a symptom, or a source of shame.
7. We Heal the LUST System Through Safe Relationships and Gentle Curiosity
Whether the client has shut down this system completely, overuses it to self-soothe, or feels lost in it, the first step is creating a space where sexuality can be explored without judgment. This includes naming feelings, respecting boundaries, and tolerating both LUST and vulnerability. With time, the LUST system can become a source of vitality, identity, and connection.

Client Handout 7: The LUST System: Your Brain's Way of Creating Affection, Closeness, and Connection

Client Handout 7: LUST System	Description
What Is LUST?	LUST is your brain's attraction system. It helps you feel drawn to people in romantic, physical, or affectionate ways. It supports bonding, closeness, and even future family-building
How Can I Tell It Is On?	You might feel pulled toward someone, want to be close, or feel curious about love or physical affection. It can come with strong feelings or questions about closeness
Why Is It So Important?	LUST helps us connect and form relationships. When respected and understood, it supports identity, emotional growth, and trust in others
What Turns It Off?	Shame, fear, trauma, or feeling unsafe can shut it down. This doesn't mean something is wrong with you, it means your system is protecting you
How Do We Respect It and Keep It Safe?	Learn about your feelings, listen to your body, and talk to safe adults about questions. Respecting yourself and others keeps LUST healthy and safe
Is Curiosity About Relationships Normal?	Yes! Wondering about dating, love, and closeness is part of growing up. It is okay to ask questions and take your time learning
What Helps It Work Best?	Feeling emotionally safe, having clear boundaries, and being respected helps this system stay healthy. Supportive relationships and honest communication matter
Can It Be Misunderstood or Hijacked?	Yes. Sometimes people confuse LUST with pressure or use it to control others. That's not healthy. LUST should always be about respect and choice
What If I'm Confused or Uncomfortable?	That's okay. These feelings can be big and sometimes hard to talk about. It helps to speak with someone you trust: a parent, counselor, or safe adult
Why Does It Matter in Counseling?	LUST helps us understand closeness, safety, identity, and connection. Talking about it can support healing, especially if someone has felt hurt or confused about touch or relationships

In addition, here are some ideas for questions that can help the client incorporate the ideas about the emotion into their everyday life:

Client Reflection Handout: My Closeness System

1 What helps you feel emotionally safe when talking about closeness or relationships?

2 Who are the trusted adults you can talk to about questions or feelings?

3 What boundaries help you feel respected and comfortable in relationships?

4 What does respectful connection look like to you?

5 What's one thing you want to learn about feelings of closeness and affection?

Draw Your Connection Self!

Use the space below to draw what feeling connected, safe, or affection looks like for you. You could draw yourself with people who make you feel respected and loved or imagine what healthy closeness looks like.

Note: A downloadable version of this handout is available via the webpage for the book at: www.routledge.com/9781041250135

References

Panksepp, J. (1998). *Affective neuroscience: The foundations of human and animal emotions*. Oxford University Press.
Panksepp, J. (2005). Affective consciousness: Core emotional feelings in animals and humans. *Consciousness and Cognition*, 14(1), 30–80.
Panksepp, J., & Biven, L. (2012). *The archaeology of mind: Neuroevolutionary origins of human emotions*. W. W. Norton.

Part III

Translating Affective Neuroscience into Clinical Practice

Chapter 13

Clinical Translation and Practice

This chapter is translational in nature as we take the neuroscience and try to use it in our practice. The tone will be much more every day and practical to facilitate the transition from academic research into what we are going to do tomorrow when we are at work. The main goal of counseling/therapy from the affective neuroscience perspective is about empowering your clients/students/self to know about how the brain–body works from a biological-evolutionary point of view and how this solid knowledge will help self-growth. We are back to believing that, with the right information and support, everyone has within themselves the capacity for great growth and adaption. Our job is to facilitate them becoming the captain of their own ship and showing them core affects via interoception will help them be strong captains indeed. So, the Affective Inventory described in this chapter has two goals: one, to educate the client about their brain–body systems and two, lead them through therapeutic exercises that help them experience their new awareness in a safe and supportive environment.

Background for Development of the Affective Inventory

I developed the Affective Inventory technique out of practical need. In the 1990s I was working in a neuropsychiatric rehabilitation hospital in Virginia. It was a unique residential facility in that the patients were children and adolescents who sustained severe brain injuries who either were admitted in coma after an extended period or had significant biopsychosocial deficits that created behavioral issues schools were not equipped to handle. The average length of stay was over a year, and I served on an interdisciplinary team that brought neuropsychology, nursing, speech, OT, PT, neurophysiatry and neuropsychiatry together to create detailed master treatment plans. The hospital also admitted youth with significant chronic illness issues (e.g. uncontrolled diabetes, gastrointestinal issues, metabolic issues, eating disorders). One thing that all the patients had in common was a disconnect between the brain and body. Patients coming out of coma not only needed to re-learn how to eat, drink, dress, and talk; they also had to learn how to gain impulse control and emotional regulation again. The connections between the core affects and the frontal lobe conscious controls were usually severely disrupted and the team had to show patients how to reconnect. For those patients with chronic illness and eating disorders,

DOI: 10.4324/9781003745686-16

they had to learn how to honor their biological and emotional needs to create a synchronous harmony between the two. In the end, we had to start each patient off with therapies to help them identify their emotions, understand their emotions, and use them to navigate their way through recovery and back at home.

At the time, there were few if any methods of treatment other than the standard behavioral approaches (much needed at the beginning of treatment because coming out of coma needed staff to walk patients through just being conscious). These methods, however, did not help us instill more advanced conscious awareness of body states (interoception) and management impulses with the patient. We needed a simple, easy to understand way of showing these young patients that different emotions need unique coping skills. We needed to link the core affects with easy-to-understand words and hopefully bring the frontal systems back into the emotions they were feeling. Without conscious understanding of what was being experienced in the body we knew that behavior would not change and that the patients would be dependent on charts and external prompts only. The later was not going to work if we wanted them to manage their behaviors independently when they got back to their home/school.

My clients were very resistant to "talk therapies" and many were too old for traditional play therapy. In fact, because most of them came to the hospital because of severe life-threatening experiences, they were quite resistant to re-living what had happened to them which was an integral part of learning how to go forward. I certainly understand their point of view! And a former mentor of mine had taught me that "resistance is not in the patient; it is in the therapist" (ouch!) and resistance was also a way of the child not engaging in therapy or the uncertain safety of rapport. So, I had to find a way of getting to know the patient, talking about deep feelings and behaviors, make the process appropriate for young patients, and make the experience attractive and enjoyable. Hence, the Affective Inventory.

In summary, the Inventory is an organized and methodical way of engaging a child/adolescent in the process of exploring a core emotion. It is designed to help the client work their way through an exploration of usually six of Panksepp's core emotions (omitting LUST in many cases because of the appropriateness of the age of the child and the setting).

Through flip chart drawings, colored pencils, guessing games, and charting the therapist asks leading questions but does not interpret or critique the responses. It is very important that the counselor reflects responses and only intervenes with suggestions (for education) at the end of the process. This is for two reasons: (1) it is very important for the client to experience their own emotions without influence from others in the room because these are deeply felt internal responses that belong to the client and should be respected (regardless of if the therapist thinks that some of the responses are incorrect or inappropriate). (2) A neutral and unconditional stance is essential if the Inventory is to be used for engaging the client in therapy. Engagement is half the battle in counseling and so safeguards must be intentional.

By the end of one session examining a core affect, the counselor will have a patient engaged in the activity, an understanding of where the patient feels different emotions in the body, a level of intensity that the patient feels the emotion, the frequency of experiencing the emotion, the existing coping skills that the patient uses in real-life situations to express the emotion, and a commitment to work on exploring the emotion and coping skills in the future. What follows is a list of the overall functions of the Inventory.

1 Builds Rapport and Reduces Resistance
Offers a developmentally appropriate, engaging entry point to connect with the child or adolescent, decreasing initial defensiveness or withdrawal.
2 Efficient Clinical Insight
Gathers a large amount of structured emotional, behavioral, and interoceptive information in a relatively short period of time.

3 Facilitates Treatment Buy-In
Provides a non-threatening way to introduce treatment goals, allowing the client to feel more invested and involved in their therapeutic process.
4 Respects the Client's Internal Experience
Supports a neutral and nonjudgmental stance, helping clinicians remain objective while affirming the client's unique perception of their emotional world.
5 Identifies Core Emotions and Body Awareness
Guides the client in recognizing primary emotional systems and how these are experienced somatically, fostering emotional literacy and interoception.
6 Integrates Brain–Body Awareness
Encourages integration of bottom-up (body-based emotional cues) with top-down (cognitive reflection and executive function) processes.
7 Enhances Emotional Self-Regulation Skills
Lays the foundation for developing personalized coping strategies based on the client's unique affective patterns and physiological responses.
8 Strengthens Therapeutic Alliance
Engaging and creative activities (drawing, mapping, storytelling) foster collaboration and trust, which are essential for meaningful therapeutic progress.
9 Provides a Developmental Bridge
Especially useful for youth who are too old for traditional play therapy but not yet ready for abstract verbal reflection.
10 Promotes Client Ownership
Encourages the client to take an active role by choosing colors, creating representations, and voicing insights thereby building internal motivation for growth.

Most important for the Affective Inventory to be a successful therapeutic method, the counselor must be sincerely humble, curious, nonjudgmental, and secure in his/her/their own beliefs about how the core emotions in work in real life. This method is a prelude for the counselor to know how the client approaches life with core emotional strategies and should assist in the development of interventions that are curated with their emotional balance in mind.

If the Inventory is client focused, then it is important to have the client do the writing. It is an act of will and therapeutic engagement. So, *they* pick the color, *they* write their answers etc. and they slowly gain ownership of the exploration of the emotion. Hopefully, this ownership becomes the first act of internalization of the information you are teaching. If nothing else, this process loudly proclaims that this exercise is about them, not what others think about them. I have found that children and youth actually enjoy the activity and ask to do it again!

Sometimes I let the client take home the flip chart page so they can look at it and digest. Other times I paste the page onto the wall in my office so that we can refer back to it during counseling. Other times I have had whole families do the exercise with each family member having their own page on the wall or white board.

These pages become a reference point and also a living document that the client gets to edit and modify as their understanding of the core emotion grows. In addition, it becomes a visual reference during counseling where the client can relate a recent real-life situation to this core drawing.

First: Do Your Own Work

Before we take each core emotion to demonstrate how things may look in your sessions with others, it is important to mention that you *do your own Affective Inventory*. Exploring and practicing on your own flipchart or workbook helps you notice your own comfort levels, emotional associations, and insights. It is essential that we do not presume we already understand these systems, particularly lesser-known ones like SEEKING, and instead remain open to discovery. Doing your own Inventory first will also allow you to experience the power of emotional affirmation and its cultural context: hopefully preventing projection of your assumptions and prior learning onto others. This is an opportunity for self-exploration, and deeper insight into ourselves and it is, frankly, fascinating!

Labels and Terms Changes

There are two reasons why the labels for the core emotions were changed for the inventory. One, because we have to translate the neuroscientific ideas to children and youth, we needed child-friendly terms and concepts. Second, the labels for the core affects have been simplified so that it is easier to talk about them on a continuum (Table 13.1). The changes are RAGE becomes ANGER, FEAR becomes SCARED, PANIC/GRIEF becomes SAD, and SEEKING and CARE remain the same because they are appropriate terms that can be easily understood. LUST remains the same because it is very difficult to find a word that better describes the system from a biological sense. Of course, clinicians will either be omitting this emotion system because of the setting, child's age, or the therapeutic need for it to be included. It is perfectly appropriate to rename or adjust the system to fit different circumstances or settings

How to Conduct the Affective Inventory

The Affective Inventory is an activity where you and the client use a flipchart and crayons (colored pencils or markers) to go through a systematic analysis of how the client experiences the different seven emotions of ANGER, SAD, SCARED, CARE, SEEKING, LUST, and PLAY. Worksheets have been included in the resources webpage for this book that are meant to be reproducible for your clients. While the actual Inventory is done on preferably flip chart paper in a playful manner, the worksheets have been included for times when the reader wants to practice, assign homework, or give out samples. It is suggested that you practice looking into your own emotional primes using these sheets or playing on a flip chart. It cannot be stated strongly enough that clinicians and educators have to know their own emotions before working with others. While many of us think that we are well educated in understanding our own and others' experiences of different emotions, it is important to understand that these *core* emotions are based in neurobiology and have specific architecture and chemistry that have not been outlined in general psychology before. Even if we understand ANGER and SAD well, we are much less likely to understand SEEKING and its interplay with other emotions. If we are not aware of our own deep emotional wiring, we will have little insight on that of others. Therefore, have fun, explore your deep emotions, test out the neurochemistry awareness for yourself, and be open to new ideas.

Table 13.1 Panksepp's Core Emotions and Affective Inventory Emotions Label

Panksepp Core Emotion Term	Affective Inventory Term	Function of the Emotion
SEEKING	SEEKING	Motivates exploration, learning, problem-solving, and engagement with the world; sustains anticipation and drive toward goals
RAGE	ANGER	Promotes self-protection, boundary setting, and protest when goals are blocked, or threats are encountered
PLAY	PLAY	Facilitates social bonding, cooperation, creativity, and development of emotional intelligence and social rules
PANIC/GRIEF	SAD	Signals loss or social separation; elicits caregiving responses and motivates reconnection and attachment repair
CARE	CARE	Supports attachment, caregiving, empathy, and social bonding; fosters prosocial behavior and emotional security
FEAR	SCARED	Promotes vigilance, risk detection, and self-preservation through defensive or avoidant behaviors
LUST	LUST	Supports bonding, reproduction, and intimacy

The Steps/Boxes

There are eight steps in the Affective Inventory, and once you have gone through them you will naturally not have to think about the details and steps of the procedure but more about the flow of your interactions with the child as you work together. Client Handout 8 is included here to illustrated where prompts and responses should be drawn on the paper.

It is very important that the client does not feel judged by you with their answers. Accept their answers with a neutral response and, even better, reflective listening. Do not openly interpret or rush to solutions as you want the child to be able to sit and digest the information. The more the child generates the more they are owning the activity and participating in self-awareness and direction. Unconditional positive regard from the counselor is paramount in this activity as it will encourage engagement and treatment adherence.

Client Handout 8: Affective Inventory

Box 1: Name of Emotion Here written in chosen color

Box 2: Place answers to "if" questions across the page here

Box 5 & 6
Place frequency here plus arrow for up or down

Box 4
Place x on the scale here about intensity of emotion

10

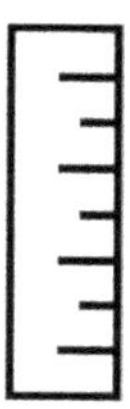

1

Box 3
Place Figure of you when you were feeling the emotion here

Box 7
What did you do about it? How did you behave?
Explain what is going on in the body-brain at this time that relates to the picture
Explain the PURPOSE of the emotion

Box 8
How did it work out? Did you get what you wanted? If not, what could be future options?

Note: A downloadable version of this as a handout is available via the webpage for the book at: www.routledge.com/9781041250135

Step/Box One: Pick a Color and Label the Emotion

Counselor Prompt:
"Have a look at these crayons. If ANGER was a color, what would it be?"
Client Task:
Client selects a colored pencil and writes their chosen emotion word at the top of the page in Box 1. This might be mad, angry, rage, etc., whatever label feels right to them.

Step/Box Two: Explore Through Interoceptive and Imaginative Inquiry

Counselor Prompt:
"If ANGER was a kind of weather, what would it be?"

Client Task: writes the response in Box 2.
Continue with prompts such as:
If ANGER was a food, what would it be?
A temperature?
A feeling on the skin?
A car?
A song or kind of music?
An animal?
A funny face, what would it look like?"

Note: Use as many creative and sensory questions as needed to help the client feel relaxed, engaged, and imaginative. Humor and playfulness can lower resistance and enhance engagement.

Step/Box Three: Draw How the Body Feels During the Emotion

Counselor Prompt:
"Think of the last time you felt ANGER. Draw a picture of yourself in that moment in Box 3".
Client Task:
Client draws a Figure representing how they felt physically while angry.
Counselor Follow-Up:
"Tell me what's going on in your body in this drawing."
Use reflective listening:
"So your arms felt heavy, and your legs were jumpy..."

Note:
Some children may be hesitant to draw. Offer stick figures if that helps. Do not rush or interpret their drawing. Let them guide the meaning and validate their explanation with reflective language.

Step/Box Four: Rate the Intensity of the Emotion

Counselor Prompt:
"If 1 is just a little bit of ANGER and 10 is a whole bunch of ANGER, what number shows how angry you were in that picture?"
Client Task:
Look at the 1–10 scale in Box 4 and circle number

Note:
Accept whatever number the child gives. Paraphrase if needed, but do not steer their answer.

Step/Box Five & Six: Frequency and Direction of Change

Counselor Prompt:
"How often do you feel this kind of anger? Every day? Once a week? Once a year?"
Client Task:
Client writes in a frequency (e.g. "3 times a week").
Counselor Prompt:
"Would you like that number to go up or down? How much?"
Client Task: circles the up or down arrow.

Note:
This is a key moment where the client expresses a desire to change their experience. It may be the first step toward identifying personal goals.

Step/Box Seven: Describe the Behavior and Context

Counselor Prompt:
"Tell me what was happening when you felt angry. What did you do?"
Client Task:
Describes the situation and their behavior.
Counselor Role:
Listen closely. Use reflective summaries such as:

"So, the little boy pushed you, it hurt, you felt hot and mad, your hands made fists, and then you pushed him back. Did I get that right?"

Note:
Help the child connect body sensations to emotional and behavioral expressions.
If appropriate, introduce gentle psychoeducation:

"When we get angry, our heart rate speeds up, and our body gets ready to protect itself. That energy can sometimes come out fast because our bodies are full of energy."

Step/Box Eight: Discuss the Outcome and Explore Alternatives

Counselor Prompt:
"How did this work out? Did you get what you wanted? Did it work for you? Let's explore that".

Client Task:
Client reflects on the outcome and possible other actions.

Counselor Role:
This step allows the child to connect their actions to the outcome. It also offers an opportunity to return to the idea that body chemistry drives emotional responses. You might say:

"Yes, when we are angry, we have a lot of energy, and we want to act to fix something, but there are lots of ways to fix things. Let's explore some of those ways".

This is also the moment to reinforce a strengths-based message: "All emotions are tools. Feeling ANGER is not wrong because we are trying to protect ourselves how we use it that matters".

You may gently offer options and lead the discussion toward problem-solving now that rapport is established. This is a powerful point where the child learns that emotions and their behaviors can be guided, not suppressed, and that asking for help or choosing a different action is both brave and smart. Use this final stage to guide the client from bottom-up sensing to top-down planning, showing them how to translate their feelings into advantageous action. The Sample Picture of Affective Inventory ANGER shows how the drawing sheet may look at the end of the session. Using the worksheets included in this book will facilitate the client transfer your training in the days following your sessions. There are also parent and educator resources to assist those who work and live with the client.

Sample Picture of Affective Inventory ANGER

Box 1: ANGER

Box 2: *chili peppers* *thunderstorms* *hot* *Red* *loud* *spiky*

Box 5 & 6
Place frequency here plus arrow for up or down

2x day ↓

Box 4
Place x on the scale here about intensity of emotion

10

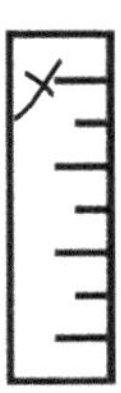

1

Box 3
Place Figure of you when you were feeling the emotion here

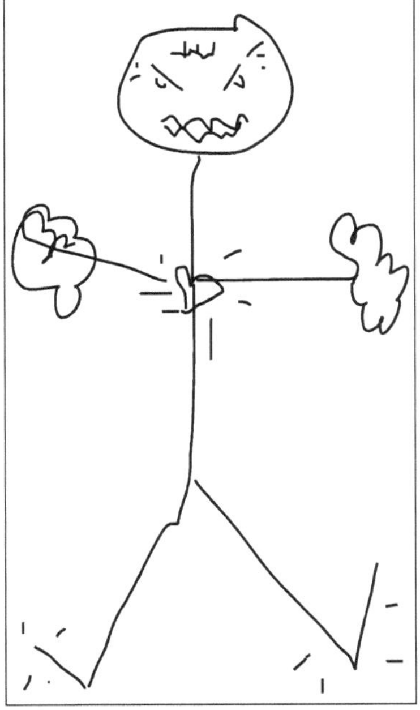

Box 7
What did you do about it? How did you behave?

"My hands went into fists, and I felt pressure in my head and my eyes were kind of closed"

"I yelled and tried to push the other person"

Box 8
How did it work out? Did you get what you wanted? If not, what could be future options?

"I got into trouble and got detention"

"I suppose I could walk away and come back later or just yell and not push"

Note: A downloadable version of this as a handout is available via the webpage for the book at: www.routledge.com/9781041250135

As with all core emotions, it's essential to revisit the Affective Inventory drawings during check-ins. Encourage children to share their charts with parents or teachers as part of their ongoing emotional learning. Completing the Inventory once is not enough; it's the repeated use and reflection with all seven core emotions that helps solidify understanding and fosters transfer into daily life.

The flip charts you create for each of the seven emotions become more than just exercises; they serve as a shared reference point between you and the child. Over time, these visual tools help deepen your insight into the child's emotional patterns and become valuable anchors for therapeutic conversations. One of the most rewarding moments in this process is when a child spontaneously refers to their own core emotion charts, using them as a framework to explain how they navigated a real-life situation. That is when you know there is a growing self-awareness and agency!

In summary, the Affective Inventory is rooted in neuropsychological rehabilitation and clinical experience. It originated from the need for a developmentally appropriate approach to teaching emotional understanding to children and adolescents recovering from brain injury or coping with chronic illness. It was naturally expanded to work with most mental health issues and in group and family sessions as well. By integrating art, metaphor, and structured inquiry, the Inventory helps clients identify where and how emotions are felt in the body, name their experiences, and link these sensations to behavior and cognition. The process emphasizes neutrality, curiosity, and client ownership, allowing children to express emotions freely without judgment. It is important to highlight how the Inventory fosters rapport, insight, emotional literacy, and self-regulation through the integration of body-based and cognitive awareness. In terms of efficiency, it is a very useful way to make the most of rapport building with clients. By the time the Inventory is completed (it can take weeks if necessary) the counselor knows the emotional foundation and experiences of the client, and the client knows that the counselor "sees" them. A good therapeutic relationship is the heartbeat of counseling (pardon the analogy) and goes a long way towards good outcomes.

Chapter 14

Summary and Conclusions

Across this book, we have moved from a narrow and often outdated view of emotions, as unpredictable, disruptive forces that need to be managed, toward a more integrated and biologically grounded understanding. Emotions, as revealed by decades of research in affective neuroscience, are neither secondary to cognition nor obstacles to be overcome. Rather, they are foundational tools that evolved to help us survive, connect, and adapt in a complex world.

At the heart of this shift is the recognition that emotions begin in the body. Our physiology, through the process of interoception, senses changes in our internal state and transmits those signals to the brain. What we call a "feeling" is not just a mental state, but a moment-to-moment interpretation of our body's internal landscape. The brain is constantly working to maintain balance, (homeostasis in the short term, allostasis in the long term) and emotions are one of its primary tools to do so.

Rather than viewing emotional experience as a disruption to be overridden by rational thinking, this book presents emotions as meaningful data. They offer insight into our needs, our boundaries, and our relationships. By understanding how these emotional systems work and how they are rooted in specific brain circuits, shaped by neurochemical messengers, and expressed through bodily states, we begin to appreciate them not as symptoms to suppress but as vital signals to respect and interpret.

Throughout the book, we have examined how the primary emotional systems identified by Jaak Panksepp (e.g. Panksepp, 1998a; Panksepp & Biven, 2012) such as SEEKING, RAGE, FEAR, PANIC/GRIEF, CARE, PLAY, and LUST form the deep structure of our affective lives. These systems drive our motivations, regulate our social behavior, and lay the groundwork for later cognitive and relational development. What emerges is a view of the self not as divided between reason and emotion, but as unified through a dynamic conversation between brain, body, and environment.

We have also explored how this understanding can be translated into clinical and educational practice. Tools such as the Affective Inventory and body-based storytelling exercises serve to bridge the science of emotion with the lived experience of clients and children. These tools emphasize co-regulation, safety, curiosity, and respect: Qualities that are essential for therapeutic growth and emotional literacy.

Importantly, this approach also acknowledges the diversity of emotional experience. While these core emotional systems are biologically shared, their expression is shaped by culture,

DOI: 10.4324/9781003745686-17

attachment, gender, neurodiversity, and lived experience. A truly compassionate and science-informed approach must honor these differences, adapting to the client's unique context while remaining anchored in the universal language of affect.

In reframing emotions as sources of allostasis, rather than problems to be solved, we open up new possibilities for healing, self-understanding, and connection. Emotional agency becomes the central goal: The ability to feel one's emotions without being overwhelmed by them, to use them as signals rather than constraints, and to respond with flexibility, clarity, and care.

This book has been an invitation to see emotions not as barriers to reason but as partners in navigating life. Through the lens of affective neuroscience, we are reminded that feelings are not failures of control: They are our first language, our internal compass, and our most exciting and enduring source of agency.

References

Panksepp, J. (1998a). *Affective neuroscience: The foundations of human and animal emotions*. Oxford University Press.
Panksepp, J., & Biven, L. (2012). *The archaeology of mind: Neuroevolutionary origins of human emotions*. W. W. Norton.

Glossary of Scientific Terms

Affective Neuroscience A branch of neuroscience devoted to understanding the neural circuits, neurochemistry, and body–brain interactions that create and regulate emotion. Founded largely by Jaak Panksepp, it emphasizes that emotions arise from subcortical systems shared across mammals and serve adaptive, survival, and social functions.

Allostasis The process by which the brain and body maintain stability through change. Allostasis involves predicting and adapting to internal and external demands rather than merely restoring balance after disruption. It extends the idea of homeostasis into flexible, anticipatory regulation.

Allostatic Load The cumulative 'wear and tear' on physiological systems that results from chronic stress or repeated efforts to maintain stability. High allostatic load contributes to physical and mental health difficulties, including inflammation, fatigue, and emotional dysregulation.

Amygdala An almond-shaped brain structure in the medial temporal lobe that plays a key role in detecting emotional salience, particularly fear and threat, and in encoding emotional memories.

Anterior Cingulate Cortex (ACC) A region of the brain that integrates cognitive, emotional, and physiological information. It helps evaluate conflicts, process pain (physical and emotional), and regulate autonomic and affective responses.

Anterior Insula A cortical area deeply involved in interoceptive awareness, the perception of internal bodily states, and the subjective experience of emotion. It acts as a bridge between bodily sensation and conscious feeling.

Bottom-Up Processing Neural and perceptual processing that begins with sensory or bodily input and moves upward through the brain. In emotion, bottom-up processing refers to how signals from the body and environment give rise to affective experiences before conscious thought.

CARE System Primary emotional systems, rooted in subcortical circuitry that supports nurturing, bonding, and social connection. Driven by oxytocin and endogenous opioids, it underlies attachment and empathy.

Cognitive Control/Top-Down Regulation The process by which higher cortical areas (especially the prefrontal cortex) influence emotional and behavioral responses originating from lower brain regions. It includes reflection, planning, inhibition, and cognitive reframing.

Default Mode Network (DMN) A set of interconnected brain regions active during rest and self-referential thought. It supports the sense of self, mental time travel, and emotional reflection.

Embodied Cognition The concept that thinking and feeling are grounded in the body's sensory and motor systems. Cognitive processes are shaped by bodily experiences, posture, and interoceptive signals.

Emotion From the Latin emovere "to move out". A biologically based affective state that mobilizes the body toward survival, adaptation, or connection. In affective neuroscience, emotions are understood as dynamic body–brain processes, not mere mental states.

Empathy The capacity to sense and resonate with another's emotional state. Neurobiologically, empathy involves the CARE and PLAY systems, mirror neurons, and interoceptive resonance.

FEAR System A primary defensive circuit that responds to perceived threats. It involves the amygdala, periaqueductal gray, and hypothalamus, mobilizing the organism for freezing, flight, or fight responses.

Homeostasis The body's tendency to maintain stable internal conditions (e.g., temperature, pH, glucose). A foundational principle in physiology, it represents short-term equilibrium; allostasis extends this concept into adaptive flexibility.

Human Affectome Project An international initiative unifying global research on affective neuroscience by mapping human emotional states and their neural correlates.

Interoception The sensing of internal bodily signals such as heartbeat, respiration, and gut tension. It is the foundation of emotional experience and self-awareness.

Limbic System A network of brain structures, including the amygdala, hippocampus, cingulate cortex, and hypothalamus, traditionally associated with emotion, motivation, and memory.

LUST System A primary emotional system driving attraction, sexual interest, and affectionate closeness. It supports bonding and reproduction through hormones such as testosterone, estrogen, and oxytocin.

Neuroplasticity The brain's ability to reorganize its structure and function in response to experience, learning, or injury. Emotional habits can be reshaped through neuroplastic processes.

Oxytocin A neurohormone produced in the hypothalamus that facilitates bonding, trust, caregiving, and relaxation. Often called the "cuddle hormone".

Panic/Grief (SAD) System A subcortical circuit associated with separation distress and social loss. It overlaps with pain pathways, explaining why social isolation and grief can be felt physically.

PLAY System Panksepp's circuitry supporting joy, social play, and learning through exploration and laughter. Essential for social competence and emotional resilience.

Predictive Coding A theory by Karl Friston proposing that the brain constantly predicts sensory input and minimizes prediction error. Emotions are viewed as signals of discrepancy between expected and actual bodily states.

Prefrontal Cortex (PFC) The front region of the brain involved in planning, reasoning, empathy, and emotion regulation. It coordinates top-down modulation of limbic responses.

RAGE System A primitive defensive circuit activated by restraint, frustration, or boundary violation. It is essential for self-protection and agency when regulated constructively.

Regulation (Emotional Regulation) The process by which the brain and body maintain emotional balance through both bottom-up (sensory, bodily) and top-down (cognitive) pathways.

SEEKING System A dopaminergic motivational circuit that energizes exploration, curiosity, and goal-directed behavior. It is the "engine of engagement" underlying motivation and learning.

Somatic Marker Hypothesis Proposed by Antonio Damasio, it posits that bodily signals ("somatic markers") guide decision-making by attaching emotional value to choices based on past experiences.

Top-Down Processing Cognitive interpretation and prediction based on prior experience, expectation, and context. In emotion, top-down control modulates bodily and limbic inputs.

Vagus Nerve A major parasympathetic nerve connecting brain and body, crucial for regulating heart rate, digestion, and social engagement. It is central to polyvagal theory and interoceptive awareness.

Index

For Product Safety Concerns and Information please contact our EU
representative GPSR@taylorandfrancis.com
Taylor & Francis Verlag GmbH, Kaufingerstraße 24, 80331 München, Germany

www.ingramcontent.com/pod-product-compliance
Ingram Content Group UK Ltd.
Pitfield, Milton Keynes, MK11 3LW, UK
UKHW050234200926
475702UK00020B/3036
* 9 7 8 1 0 4 1 2 5 0 1 3 5 *